CW00684898

# The Colburn School

# The Colburn School

## THE LEGACY OF RICHARD D. COLBURN

~

**Richard D. Colburn**

Colburn School
2016

Copyright © 2016 Colburn School
All rights reserved.

ISBN: 0692615105
ISBN 13: 9780692615102
Library of Congress Control Number: 2016900498
Colburn School, Los Angeles, CA

# Contents

# Preface

~

THE OCTOBER 7, 1998 ISSUE of the *New York Times* featured an article entitled, "When Wealth Promotes Love of Music: Los Angeles School Gets a New Home and a National Goal." The article began prosaically: "Eighty years ago, when Richard D. Colburn was growing up…in San Diego, his mother surprised him on his seventh birthday with a violin and a bow and took him to have his first lesson." The story recounts how that gift of a violin begat a life-long interest in music, which, when matched with remarkable success in business, led Richard D. Colburn to both a vision for a music school in Los Angeles and the financial resources to fulfill his aspiration. With that introduction, the article arrives at the "news": the inauguration of the new home of the Colburn School of Performing Arts across the street from the Walt Disney Concert Hall in downtown Los Angeles. Mentioned, too, are plans to expand the School with the addition of a four-year, tuition-free, college-level conservatory. The stated intent is to match established national institutions like the Julliard School in New York and the Curtis Institute of Music in Philadelphia.

A decade later, the Colburn School was again the subject of a lengthy article in the *New York Times*. The January 6, 2008 issue reported, "A Conservatory Stresses the Music, Eliminates the Bills." Plans were fulfilled. A conservatory was established at the Colburn School in 2003, and a handsome new building was added to house it: twelve stories tall, replete with classrooms, practice rooms, an orchestra rehearsal hall, a recital hall, and a cafeteria and housing for up to 130 students. The conservatory offers a bachelor's degree in music performance and two graduate programs, a master's degree in music and an artist's diploma for students seeking to broaden their repertory. There is also a less-structured professional studies certificate for those on the verge of a career in music. The Colburn School was reported by the *New York Times* to have superb facilities, an excellent faculty, and an endowment provided by its benefactor—Richard D. Colburn—that enables students to be offered not only a tuition-free program, but also "room and board." A student is quoted in the article as saying, "When we came to Colburn, we had earthly concerns taken away; we could focus just on music." (Those enrolled in the community division, primarily children who attend after school for instruction, do pay for classes.) The Colburn School was held to have achieved early success, already attracting the finest young musicians, not just from the United States, but from throughout the world, especially from Europe and Asia.

Richard D. Colburn died in 2004 at the age of ninety-two. He was my "Uncle Richard." He was always kind to me and I admired him. Even when I was just a boy, his success in business was readily apparent and so, too, was his deep engagement with classical music. Just a couple of years before he died, I was his guest at the Metropolitan Opera for a performance of one of the operas that comprise Wagner's *Ring Cycle*. At the end of the performance, my Uncle Richard's face was wet with tears. He certainly had heard the opera many times, but he was still enraptured by it. Those with whom he played string quartets were also impressed that he would at times be so enthralled by beautiful passages of music that they were playing that he would shed tears. Yet, in business, Uncle Richard was coldly objective, analytical, and piercing. "Business was business." He was soft-spoken and unpretentious, but always focused and intense.

Uncle Richard avoided publicity. He would quote a maxim of his father's—of my grandfather: "Fools' names and fools' faces often appear in public places." Still, Uncle Richard, at the urging of many, consented to give his name to the Colburn School. He was more than the benefactor. The school, in its scale and in its ambition, is very much his dream. And he not only had a dream; he also had the means to make it come alive. I remember hearing from him years ago, as he drove like Niki Lauda on the Los Angeles freeways, how unfortunate it was that the West Coast of the United States did not have a single music school equal to that of the great music schools on the East Coast. He wanted to correct that omission—and he did. It is fitting that the Colburn School bears the name of its founder.

This book is the memoir of Richard D. Colburn. Its style and design evoke the brilliant title of Vladimir Nabokov's autobiography, *Speak, Memory*. My Uncle Richard was persuaded by friends to record the outline of his life. He was interviewed at length and these interviews were recorded and later transcribed. Thus, he just drew on his memory, only rarely consulting either an atlas or a bit of correspondence that he had saved. Memories are murky and imperfect. What do we remember and why? Answers inevitably vary by individual. Still, memories are important. A memory is more than a repository: it guides us, continually shaping decisions. Reading Uncle Richard's memoir makes it clear that his life as an adult, for example, was profoundly shaped by his childhood, including not only by his mother's gift of a violin, but also by his father's monasticism. I will never forget at the close of the inauguration ceremony for the Colburn School leading my father to his brother, who was encircled by courtly men and women. My father, in his late eighties, was just bawling. Uncle Richard asked me, "What is the matter with your father?" I replied, as calmly as I could, "He says mother would be so proud." Uncle Richard, too, lost his composure and fled the fawning crowd.

The interviews of Richard D. Colburn began in the spring of 2001 and stretched until December of 2002. He thus was eighty-nine when the interviews began and ninety-one when they concluded. There were eleven interviews, which resulted in over thirty hours of taped reminiscences. Others were interviewed, too, including family members, friends, and colleagues in business. The interviews were conducted by JoAn Kunselman. Assistance in the project was also provided by Robert Attiyeh, Gene Krieger, William Myers, and Allison Sampson. A manuscript emerged, but it was sprawling and unwieldy. It languished. I offered to edit it, being an academic and the author of a number of books published by august university presses. My offer was accepted and I have done what I thought sensible.

The work remains in the first person singular, in a conversation-style, complete with contractions. I reordered passages to make the work more "linear" and cogent, and I deleted passages either because they were incomplete or vague, or because they were repetitious. I noticed, as I worked, that Uncle Richard was most drawn to recounting early memories, and less interested in what was fresher, more immediate. I wonder if this proclivity to speak of the distant past was from nostalgia or because he concluded that these earlier experiences were more decisive in shaping him, in making him into who he was and guiding him throughout his life.

Uncle Richard focused on two subjects—business and music. His long life spanned most of the twentieth century, sometimes called "the long century" for all of the political calamities that wreaked such havoc. However, there is next to no mention of the great political dramas that unfolded throughout Uncle Richard's life. Like many men of his generation, Uncle Richard was emotionally reticent, and there is little here either of his personal life, perhaps because he thought it was impolite to speak of it, or maybe because he assumed it would not be of interest to others. The twentieth century is sometimes also referred to as the "American century," because of the extraordinary economic growth and prominence of the United States. Here Uncle Richard's tale makes a contribution: he offers a view of what some in the academy call the "micro-foundation" of this economic growth, the reordering of economic activity into that paragon of scale and efficiency, the "firm." Now and then I teach as a visiting professor at a management school, and I cannot help but conclude that some of the chapters here could profitably be read by students seeking to do business in the fiercely competitive twenty-first century.

While Richard D. Colburn had a sense for business, his passion was for music. Throughout his life, he was nurtured by music. The Colburn School is his gift of gratitude to the joy music brought to his life.

Forrest D. Colburn
New York City
January 26, 2016

# CHAPTER 1

# Childhood and Family

*Our little Richard boy was born about twenty minutes before twelve noon Saturday morning, June 24, 1911. He weighed seven pounds and was not at all fat, but was called a strong baby. His eyes were blue, his hair, red, and his hands and feet, large for his size. He was not at all red, but very, very pink. After his long naps, he would stretch so hard his little fists would shake, which would always make the nurse and me laugh.*

My mother, Daisy Dunton Colburn, kept a diary through the first year and one half of my life. The above entry, from when I was six weeks old, shows the pleasure she was experiencing in me, her firstborn.

Her entry on Christmas Day 1911, when I was six months old, reveals the nurturing home in which I had arrived:

*Mother and Aunt Kate, my mother's older half-sister, both say he is the liveliest baby there ever was in this house—and they ought to know. When held up so he can just touch his feet to the floor or table, he makes his feet go so fast it looks as if he were dancing or prancing like a colt. We all agree that we are paying him too much attention, but it just seems as if we cannot help it because he is so jolly and inviting with all his smiles and talk.*

When I was over a year old, my mother wrote:

> *It would be hard to say who makes the most fuss over him: Mrs. Wendt, Kate, or his father Cary. He never wants to come to me from either of them and will shake his head quite emphatically, just as he does when he has had enough to eat and we offer him more....Cary is at home and takes nearly all the care of Richard, which is giving me a very easy time, for which I am thankful every day. [Richard] is surely the sunshine of this household—so happy, and loving, and full of fun—always ready with his smile and baby chatter—a most friendly little fellow.*

I was born in Carpentersville, Illinois, on the Fox River. This village is about thirty-five miles west and slightly to the north of Chicago. It is about straight west from Winnetka, a mile north of Dundee, and about six miles north of Elgin. I was born in the same home where my mother had been born; it was the home of my grandmother, Mary Roberts Dunton. Mary Roberts was of Welsh descent, and she married Delos Dunton, who was of Scottish origin. They named their daughter, my mother, Daisy Dunton. Delos Dunton's gravestone in Carpentersville indicates he was born in 1833, but it does not state where he was born. He emigrated from Broughty Ferry, Scotland, which is the port for Dundee. He came to Dundee, Illinois, from which he later moved north up the Fox River to Carpentersville.

My paternal grandfather, Richard Oldfield Colburn, was of English descent. He was a very successful farmer in Eureka County, in a little town called Secor. Over the years, he bought other farms so that he had a farm to leave to each of his nine children: five boys (William, John, Cary, Cecil, and Byron) and four girls (Mary, Geneva, Leona, and Rosalia), plus two or three farms to leave to his widow. His wife, my paternal grandmother, was Julia Manor, who was of French-Canadian origin. She lived to be eighty-three. My paternal grandfather died earlier. I have forgotten from what cause.

Three of my father's four brothers went on to be farmers themselves. My father's oldest brother William owned a grain elevator in Secor and had some other business interests. Another brother, Uncle John, inherited the family farm that I visited as a boy. I can remember being bathed in a big galvanized iron tub on the floor in the kitchen at Uncle John's house with my two younger brothers. Uncle Cecil had a very nice house on his farm. He had two children, Caurine and Lowell. His wife's name was Minnola.

My father, Cary Richard Colburn, graduated from Harvard *cum laude* in 1895 and, the following year, he became principal of the high school in Superior, Wisconsin. He stayed for a year. My father then went back to Harvard where, in 1899, he earned his law degree. Then he went to work for a law firm in Chicago named Holt, Wheeler & Sidley, now known as Sidley Austin. He found the law profession to be not at all what he wanted. The firm had him back in a "bullpen" researching cases and summarizing decisions, which he'd review with one of the partners. Occasionally, my father was sent back to get the book in which the case was cited so that the partner could read firsthand the decision and have some of the facts in the case. My father left law practice and got a job teaching at Eureka College in Woodford County, Illinois. This college is where later President Ronald Reagan studied and played on the football team. Eureka was the county seat.

The same year my father started teaching at Eureka College, my mother also joined the faculty. She taught art. They met at a new-faculty dinner given by Mr. Hieronymus, who was then the president of Eureka College, and whom I met later. Subsequently, I think in 1901 or 1902, my father went to Japan, where he had a teaching position. He proposed marriage to my mother by mail from Japan. He came back after a year, they married, and he took her back with him to Japan, where she taught art. They crossed the Atlantic by boat, traveled by train to Moscow, and took the Trans-Siberian Railway from Moscow to Vladivostok. Then, from Harbin, Manchuria, they crossed the Sea of Japan. They stayed for five years. My mother wanted children, but she desired for them to be born in America, so they came back to the United States in 1910. In 1911, I was born.

In 1910, when they came back to Carpentersville, they moved in with my grandmother in the big house on the hill where I was born, and where my mother had been born, too. It was the largest and best-situated house in Carpentersville. My grandfather, Delos Dunton, had been the head of a company called the Illinois Iron and Bolt Company, which made plowshares and different kinds of wagon hardware. He also raised Morgan carriage horses on a farm he owned in Kansas. He brought the horses to an area north of Carpentersville, where he had them broken in for the horse carriage trade. In addition to running the Illinois Iron and Bolt Company, he also had some timberland and swampland down in Tennessee. It was there, wading through the swamps, where he contracted yellow fever, from which he died prematurely. My grandmother lived to be eighty-six.

When my father came back from Japan, he sold the farm he had inherited from his father and put the money into a membership on the Chicago Board of Trade, where he specialized in grain futures. From then on, he made a living by gambling in futures. He had grown up on a farm, knew farming, and he knew the effects of weather. Speculation was the source of the family's income. I have had a disdain ever since for people who make their money trading and speculating in stocks and bonds, grain futures, metals, pork bellies, or other commodities because they don't perform any socially useful function. Still, one can argue about what they add to the stability of the market. I can understand that if you are producing flour you need to have a place from which to buy additional wheat for future delivery to keep your mills going. The same can be said if you are grinding corn, feeding corn to hogs, or fattening cattle or hogs in feedlots.

My mother had bunions because of a foot problem caused by her wearing high-heeled shoes from back before I can remember. I remember her always wearing flat-heeled shoes, and she spoke to me about the importance of wearing sensible shoes.

My earliest recollections are of chasing geese on the property of my grandmother's daughter, Kate, who was from a marriage previous to my grandmother's marriage to Delos Dunton. I also have a recollection of visiting my paternal Aunt Mary, the older sister of my father, in St. Petersburg, Florida. I can remember the steep steps from the street up to the house, and I can remember a horse-drawn, ice cream vendor wagon coming along, with the driver ringing a big bell held in his hand. From that day to this, I have been a great lover of ice cream: "I scream for ice cream!"

When I was three and a half years old, in December 1914, my parents moved to San Diego, California. The Panama-California Exposition was being held in Balboa Park. We stayed for a few months in Ocean Beach, which is on the ocean side of Point Loma. My father bought a home on Meade

Avenue. I remember a little bit about living in Ocean Beach, and I remember Meade Avenue. I remember taking my youngest brother Price out of his baby carriage and getting into the carriage myself on Meade Avenue. The carriage rolled over a wall and dumped me on the sidewalk. I received an injury to my forehead that required some stitches. There is a small scar I carry to this day, but it is now hardly discernible.

I was the eldest of what my mother said were "three lovely boys": Richard, William, and Price. William was born December 18, 1912, and Price, August 6, 1914, so William was about one and a half years younger than I am, and Price was about three years younger than I am. I remember being driven by car to kindergarten at the Jefferson Grammar School on 28th Street, the street where my father had bought a new house that we would move into when it was completed. The car we were riding in was hit and turned on its side by another automobile. It was my first experience of an automobile accident and, actually, my worst accident ever.

I have heard stories about my kindergarten days, and I have dim recollections of doing what these stories report. Instead of playing on the playground, I went to peek in the first grade room to see what was on the blackboard: I was curious about what was going on in the other classes. I was moved ahead rather rapidly in grade school, skipping 2A, 3A, 4A, and 6A, the first half of grades 2, 3, 4, and 6. So I finished grammar school two years ahead of the normal age. Then I went to Roosevelt Junior High School, to which I rode my bicycle every day. It was probably a ride of two or three miles. I carried my lunch in a paper bag.

On my seventh birthday, my mother gave me a violin with a bow and a case, which she bought for ten dollars. She took me to have my first violin lesson. I have no recollection of expressing an interest in studying the violin, and I don't remember ever having heard a violin played. My mother practiced the violin with me, which I loved. She learned along with me. I don't remember what led to this incident, but I remember well lying on the floor on my back crying because I was having some problems in my practice. My teacher was Mr. Rinkle, and he had a shingle, a sign hanging on the front of his house, that stated, "Teacher of violin, piano, mandolin, banjo, and guitar." I would call him today a jack of all trades, master of none.

I was a victim of poor music teaching. When I was in high school, the conductor at San Diego High School, Mr. Nino Marcelli, told me that I wasn't good enough to be first or second violinist in a string quartet composed of members of the orchestra, which he wanted to form. He didn't need to tell me; I knew I wasn't first or second best. He did tell me that if I would switch to viola, I might be better than any of the violists he then had. So I switched, and since I was better than any of the other violists, I became a member of the first string quartet that was established at the school. The school has since been torn down. It was at the southwest corner of Balboa Park. The school was in a beautiful, old grey stone building.

I was red-headed, freckled, and if what was said was true—I don't know that it was—my ears stuck out. I was teased about my red hair and was called "red-headed woodpecker" and a sissy because I carried a violin case. I practiced every morning after breakfast for a half-hour before going off to school. When I started, I took two lessons a week. Later, I took one lesson a week. From the time I was seven until I was fourteen, I practiced thirty minutes a day after breakfast before going off to school.

We had a chicken coop with chickens in the backyard. Occasionally, my father would kill a chicken by chopping its head off. Then he would dip the carcass in hot water to facilitate pulling the feathers off the body. I remember him killing and cleaning chickens. We also had cats; at one time we had thirteen cats. We had a dog, named Blackie. Once when he was on the west side of 28th Street in front of the house and I was across the street on my bicycle, I called Blackie. Blackie started to run across the street to me and was hit by an automobile—and killed. I had a little funeral for Blackie. I buried him on the north side of the house and put a cross I made on his grave.

My brothers also took music lessons. William studied the piano for seven years and then had a choice of taking piano lessons or doing some household chores. He preferred doing chores rather than practicing the piano, so he gave up the piano as a child, and I don't think he has touched it since. Price played the violin, but he didn't care for it and gave it up. He also took on additional household chores.

I can remember helping my mother with laundry, hanging the clothes on the clothesline, taking them down, and turning the wringer to squeeze water out of the clothes. I liked helping my mother. I remember taking the rugs out of the house, putting them on the lawn upside down, beating them to get the dirt out of them, and then taking them back in and putting them on the floor. I would dust the stairs from the first floor to the upstairs. Our downstairs had a living room with a wood-burning fireplace, a dining room, a kitchen, a laundry room with a water closet and a washbasin, a breakfast room, and a sort of library room. We had a housekeeper named Ina Goetzke.

At one point, my two brothers and I all slept in one bedroom, and there was a bathroom on the second floor. We slept in three little single beds. I can remember in my earliest childhood playing marbles, but I was never as good as my brother William. We also used to play handball, and I would hit the ball by hand against the garage door. Again, William was a better handball player than I was. But I could run faster than he could, and I could jump higher in the high jump, and jump further in the running broad jump or the standing broad jump. I could run faster than either William or Price.

One of the most dramatic events in my early days at Jefferson Grammar School was my wanting five cents to buy a Cluster Ruff candy bar made by the Bishop Candy Company in San Diego. During her life with my father, my mother literally never had any money in her purse. I sat out in the alley behind the house crying, and finally she was able to get a nickel from my father for me to buy that candy bar. Similarly, I remember very well one morning my father standing in what we called the sunroom, a room in the front of the house on the second floor, which was an early add-on. He was standing in his nightshirt, holding his watch in his hand, telling me to hurry or I would be late to school. I remember thinking, "Goddammit, you're there in your nightshirt trying to rush me off, and all the other fathers on the street have already long since left home to go to work." I always resented my father's failure to work like other fathers did.

During my boyhood, our neighbors two doors to the south were the Justice family. Mr. Justice was in the honey distribution business in San Diego County. At that time, he was a significant distributor of honey. I would sell honeycomb door-to-door for him to make a little pin money. So I learned the importance of sales, and that's where you make the money. Of course, a lot of people are in sales and don't make money. You need to manage your expenses. But, in that honey job, you didn't have very many expenses to manage.

We had the only Ford on 28th Street. At that time, 28th Street ran from the Pershing Drive exit at the southwest corner of Balboa Park diagonally northeast to another corner of Balboa Park. It was about four miles from my house to downtown. Two doors to the north of us was the Grace family. The Grace family had two girls, and the Justice family, two or three boys and one girl. They are the only neighbors whose names I remember now. Automobiles on our street included Wills-Saint Claire, Jordan, Franklin, Marmon, Pierce-Arrow, Maxwell, Dodge Gardner, Chandler, and Hudson. But we, the Colburns, had the only Ford, and I resented that. We had an upright piano, whereas the neighbors had baby grand pianos, which I thought were much more attractive. My family celebrated Christmas only modestly, and I felt deprived. We'd have a little tree, about one and a half or two feet high. I remember stringing cranberries and popcorn and putting them on the tree. Any decoration we'd put on the tree we made ourselves.

That sense of deprivation in childhood resulted in my wanting later to live well, in comfort. For example, I always have had not just good cars, but the best—Cadillacs and Mercedes. I also had two Rolls-Royces, both of them convertibles, because I loved convertibles. I loved to drive around with the top down. I'll never forget driving from Milwaukee down to Winnetka, Illinois with the top down in a brand new Thunderbird. The first year the Thunderbird came out, I bought one. My son Richard went up to Milwaukee with me to get that Thunderbird, and we rode back to Winnetka. It was freezing cold and it snowed. I had icicles in my hair, but I loved it.

My mother had a small income of her own from dividends from the Illinois Iron and Bolt Company. My father had custody of her checks, wrote them, and my mother signed them. My mother always paid for my music lessons. My father, as far as I know, never paid for a lesson. I had a cheap violin. I said it was "Notoni Bastardi" violin, a "no-toned bastard." I remember in my early years being loaned a somewhat better violin than I was then using. I was pleased to have the use of this violin.

This act of generosity motivated me in the late 1940s, when I had a little more money than I needed for myself and my family, to start collecting instruments played with a bow—violins, violas, and cellos—which I lent to young people. Handled like books in a circulating library, the instruments had to be returned at the time the young people abandoned their studies, launched their professional careers, or reached the age of twenty-five.

I remember an experience I had after studying with my first teacher, Mr. Rinkle. I had some lessons with Russell Keeney, who had graduated from the Yale School of Music. Russell took Joe Kirshbaum, one of his other pupils, and me to the home of Mr. Grainger, a wealthy man in San Diego who had made his money by "grubstaking" some miners in the Gold Rush, and who owned a Stradivarius violin. I remember going to his home. He walked over to a big breakfront, unlocked it, took the Stradivarius violin out, and held it out in his two hands. I thought he was handing it to me, but as I reached out to take the violin, he pulled it back. He would not let me hold it or touch a bow to the strings. I thought, "You son-of-a-bitch. Stradivarius didn't make this instrument to be locked up in a breakfront like you have it. It was made to be played." I never forgot that experience. I think this incidence was also a factor in motivating me to lend to young musicians the instruments that I later collected.

When I was sixteen, I joined the musicians' union, the American Federation of Musicians, of which Mr. Petrillo was then the president. I turned in my union card after seven years. I had learned that I couldn't earn enough money as a violist to satisfy my material desires. So, I abandoned music as a career and planned other activities.

In my youth, I was always the underdog, or at least I felt like I was the underdog. I was striving to gain recognition, so one does lots of stupid things. I never will forget something I did while playing in a San Diego high school orchestra when I think I was probably twelve or thirteen years old. Some of the older fellows had a Kotex with a pin in it and they persuaded me to hang it on the skirt of a bass player. I could just reach out—she was standing right next to my left arm—and I did it. Of course, word got around. Soon I was called into the principal's office. I didn't know what a Kotex was. I had no notion in the world. A Mr. Perkins was the principal. There were almost 500 teenagers in my grade, and so about 2,000 teenagers in the high school. Mr. Perkins made me apologize to the girl for what I regard now as a petty offense, and I was humiliated and hurt. Mr. Perkins also called my mother and told her what I had done. She expressed her disappointment in me.

What I learned from that experience in the orchestra and the principal's office was how stupid I was to do something that I did not understand. In other words, I didn't blame the fellows who made the suggestion to me. I blamed myself. I learned to be sure you know what you're doing before you do it.

I never had a date in all the time I was in high school. I never learned to swim, so when the class had a class day out at the beach, I didn't go because I couldn't swim. When they had a prom, I didn't go because I didn't know how to dance. I was a social outcast.

In those days in California, one could get a driving license at fourteen, so when I was fourteen, I got a driver's license. I graduated from high school two days before my fifteenth birthday. The fall of that year, I went to the California State Normal School in San Diego. I was miserable there. As a fifteen-year-old, I was the youngest student. The other students were about seventeen to twenty-three. I was totally isolated from and ignored by the other students. I was very lonely. Shortly after that time, fortunately, I made a little money by teaching violin. I had some students that Mr. Rinkle referred to me. My mother and father were divorced about that time. My father went off again to Japan to teach.

I have some memories of my brothers, William and Price, from those early years. My brother William went one year to Antioch College, the college I also attended, and while there he worked as a stock boy in the Rike-Kumler Department Store in Dayton, Ohio. He pushed one of those carts around, delivering new merchandise to various departments in the store, and he picked up merchandise from the various departments that had been sold and needed to be delivered. It was William's first winter in the snow, and it was his first exposure to the real world. He hated it. He hated what he saw of the working world so much that he told my father he didn't want to go to college anymore. William asked my father to just give him the same amount of money he gave me to go to Antioch, and he'd put it into the stock market. He said he'd work and would not take a nickel out of the market. I think it was either 1931 or 1932 when William went into the stock market and got the same amount of money each year as I did from our father, who was then in Japan. William put the money into the stock market and didn't take any out until, I think, 1946. William made his living by playing in bridge clubs. The bridge club where he played was very close to the E. F. Hutton brokerage office. He would have breakfast in a little restaurant or cafeteria, and then go out the back door, across the alley, to the E. F. Hutton brokerage firm and watch the board. At that time they marked up the stock prices in chalk on a blackboard. He'd be there for the opening of the market in New York, or soon after the opening. Then he'd go to the bridge club, play bridge, and come back occasionally during the day between bridge games to see how the market was doing.

My brother Price married quite early. Price was handsome as a teenager, and the beauty queen of the class was his girlfriend. I remember Price having been sent to spend a year of high school in Japan. Then he married Wilma right out of high school, I think at the age of nineteen. I didn't attend his wedding. They were married for thirty-five years and had two children, Randy and Whitney Ann. Price divorced in the 1960s, so he would have been in his fifties.

William married Elizabeth and they had three boys. One of these boys was named Forrest after a cousin of my mother's, whom my mother married some years after she and my father were divorced (the other two boys were named Henry and William Junior). My mother's second husband, Forrest, had the general store in Carpentersville. He sold dry goods, groceries of all kinds, thread, needles, yarn and knitting needles, among other things. My mother died in a hospital in Elgin,

Illinois, in early January 1943. She had a small benign growth in her intestine, and the operation was a success, but she died soon after the surgery from peritonitis. It was before antibiotics and other drug treatments that would have saved her. You seldom hear of anyone dying anymore of peritonitis.

My father died at the age of eighty-four in Cambridge, Massachusetts, just after he had attended his 60th college class reunion. He had been feeling poorly, wrote me a letter in a birthday card, took it to the mailbox, and died of a ruptured aorta within hours. The letter I received, dated June 21, 1955, includes these passages:

> *I got ready and went to the Memorial Chapel at three-thirty to hear President Pusey tell the graduating class to free their minds from their imprisoned walls and join the crusade of educated men to free all mankind. I felt that I had come back to the Harvard that I had known in the 19th century, when, as President Eliot had said, "Harvard, the oldest, the richest, and the freest university in the United States." I was happy, and I was able to attend all of the festivities of my class in its 60th reunion, ending with the class dinner Thursday night at the Harvard Club in Boston.*
>
> *I can never repay you, Richard, for all you have done and are doing for me. I often think of what an old man in Eureka said to me as I passed his house as I was pulling you in your little go-cart. He was sitting out in his yard as I passed and you were very happy—all smiles as you were riding along, seeing the sights of Eureka, your new hometown for the summer. He called out: "Do you think he will ever do that for you?" I replied, "I don't know—that thought never occurred to me." So it is, a parent never thinks of ever being repaid for what he does for*

*his child. He casts his bread upon the waters and, after many years, it comes back. Life does have its compensations, and the greatest are one's children. What would life be to an old man like me without children?*

*Have a happy birthday. You are now forty-four; about the age I was when I was giving you a ride in Eureka in your little go-cart. My best love to all. Papa*

# CHAPTER 2

# An Education and a Start

~

AFTER GRADUATING FROM HIGH SCHOOL, I spent one year at the San Diego State Normal School. That was the time when, to get a teaching job, you almost had to have a degree from a normal school, which taught teachers how to teach. The following year, I taught violin, and the next year, I played in the San Diego Symphony. I played in its inaugural concert and also played for the Oratorio Society in San Diego. I think there were four oratorios each season. I remember the San Diego Symphony had its summer series in Balboa Park, called "Symphonies under the Stars." I loved playing those concerts. It was great to play outdoors on the beautiful San Diego evenings.

The second year after my debacle at the San Diego State Normal, I took a job as an office boy with the *San Diego Sun,* a Scripps Howard afternoon newspaper. This job as an office boy was my first major exposure to business. My role was to receive telephone calls from subscribers complaining about a newspaper having been thrown into the bushes or onto a wet lawn, about the delivery boy having stopped up the street to play ball with some of his friends, or that the delivery boy forgot them. In other words, I was taking the complaints and passing them on to the district managers who supervised the boys and had the responsibility to follow up and see that the customer's needs were met and the proper apologies delivered. Early on in that experience, one of the district circulation managers was fired, and I was given his job. In other words, I was then responsible for the boys giving service. My business experience started.

My initial position as an office boy was the first job offer I had received, and I took it. I don't remember how I was offered that job. I was sixteen or seventeen years old at the time. I know I was eighteen when I left it to go to Antioch College. The main lesson I learned from my first job was that there's nothing more important than service, to fulfill the needs of your customer or your client, whomever he or she might be. I learned that lesson because I was the one that heard the complaints. For the boys, the more customers they had, the more money they made. They basically were in business for themselves because they were charged a certain amount for the papers and then they charged their customers a higher amount. They had to collect the money themselves, so they were really in business. If they had an angry customer, a "deadbeat," or bought more papers than they needed, they lost money. So they were motivated to do well, at least to an extent.

I learned, too, that circulation of newspapers tends to go down during the summer, at least in San Diego, when people go away for summer holidays. What was then called the Audit Bureau of Circulation audited a newspaper's circulation to be sure that they were meeting the guarantees in their advertising contracts. So there was always a drive to get new subscribers, to replace those who moved away. Each year, the seven boys who got the largest number of new subscribers were given a free boat trip to San Francisco. The district manager whose boys got the highest average number of new subscribers got to take that trip along with the boys. I won in 1929, and so that summer I went by boat to San Francisco. There were two boats, the Harvard and the Yale; we went up on one boat and came back on the other.

I was like an older brother to the paperboys on that trip. They were younger than I was. One night after a movie in San Francisco, we were coming back to the Sir Francis Drake Hotel. We were walking along on Market Street, and there was an Emporium Department Store that had an inside arcade with showrooms on four sides. The floor had a smooth polished-stone finish. One could run and slide on it, and that night I did just that. Unfortunately, I had one hand out and broke a plate glass window after sliding into it. For years, I could see the stitches in my wrist. We were chaperoned on this trip by the circulation manager and I can remember my humiliation in having to tell my boss what I had done, and in having the boys know how stupid I was. I'll never forget that embarrassing incident. At times I was made to feel I was very bright and other times I myself concluded I was stupid.

I shouldn't have been doing that sliding and enticing the boys to join me. It was fun, but I should've set a better example for those boys. I should have had dignity and poise. Still, the wider lesson I learned from my work with the newspaper is that sales make jobs, and sales bring rewards. I recognized the importance of selling.

Just after my eighteenth birthday in 1929, my violinist friend, Joe Kirshbaum, and I drove east across the country. I dropped Joe off in Dayton, Ohio, which was eighteen miles from Antioch College, and he took a bus from there to New

Haven to begin his freshman year at the Yale School of Music. I went to Antioch College.

Horace Mann, the father of public education in America, who had a great belief in coeducation, founded Antioch College in Yellow Springs, Ohio. He knew that coeducation would never go over at that time in the Boston area where he started out, so he went out into what was the new West with open minds and founded Antioch College. Antioch was a pioneer in putting men and women together in the classroom. However, because Antioch didn't manage its money well, it went bankrupt and closed up in the early twenties. Arthur Morgan, who was later chairman of the Tennessee Valley Authority, had never gone to college, but was a self-taught hydraulic engineer. At the time of Antioch's demise, Morgan and his firm were engaged in constructing a series of dams in the Little Miami River to prevent the flooding of downtown Dayton. A number of businessmen in Dayton knew Morgan and were involved in that flood-control project. Morgan preached his views about education, so they said, "Morgan, why don't you go out and run Antioch College?" And he did.

Under Antioch's program at that time, students alternated between study and work. Students worked twenty-six weeks a year, went to school twenty weeks a year, and had six weeks of vacation—one week at Christmas and five weeks in the summer. Two students held down a job together. While one was in school, the other was on the job. Over a weekend, one student would go from school to the job while his co-op partner would return from the job to school.

My decision to go to Antioch College was really made for me by my father. He had been a subscriber to the *Antioch Notes*, a monthly pamphlet that Morgan wrote. He was sold on the work-study program and persuaded me to go. I doubt that my father saw Antioch's work-study program as compatible with my interest in business and working. For me, my father was a "goof-off." To this day, I resent that my father didn't make better use of his life. In any case, he persuaded me that going to Antioch was the thing to do, because, after my year at the Normal School in San Diego, I was miserable. I didn't know where I wanted to go.

When I arrived at Antioch in September 1929, the so-called extramural department that finds jobs for the students asked me what I wanted to do, and I said, "Well, I would like to be in advertising." One thing I had learned from my experience at the newspaper was that the big money was not in writing editorials or news items, or running the presses, or delivering the papers. It was in selling advertising. So Antioch got a job for me at Westinghouse Electric at its headquarters and executive offices in East Pittsburgh, Pennsylvania. At Westinghouse, I was exposed to what struck me as a tremendous waste of human resources, all the way around. I would walk through the plant and see men standing around talking. The whole pace of things was wrong. I would see the president arriving, driven up in a big car. He didn't get there at eight o'clock in the morning like the rest of us. I think that experience was the beginning of my realization of the importance of being the first employee to arrive and the last to leave. I thought: "What the hell! How can the president know if people are on the job if he's not there himself? And how does he know they stick with their jobs if he leaves before they leave?"

I also found out very quickly in that year that advertising was not what I wanted at all. I lost interest in advertising. Fortunately, I was back at Antioch after my first five weeks.

However, since under the Antioch program two students hold down a job together, I had to stick with that Westinghouse job for a year. I couldn't just leave.

When I first came to Antioch, my faculty adviser was Professor Dave Magruder, who taught accounting. I didn't know what accounting was, except I had seen an ad in a magazine saying, "Be an accountant—earn $3,000 a year." I saw Professor Magruder the first day I arrived at Antioch. I was casting around for electives, and he said, "Why don't you take a course in accounting with me?" I said, "Fine." So I did!

In addition to being the accounting professor, Mr. Magruder had the responsibility for overseeing the student bookstore in the main building on campus. So, in my second year, I was made the student manager of the bookstore with Scotty Wilcox, a senior, as my co-op manager. The manager earned a percentage of the profit over a fixed return on capital. You were restricted to a ten-percent markup on books and a carefully defined set of academic supplies. You made your money by selling books other than those required for classes. We sold all kinds of books, including the Old and New Testaments of the Bible. We sold school stationery, school rings, pins, school emblem stickers to put on baggage, sweatshirts, socks, tennis shoes, fountain pens, pencils, erasers, paper, tennis rackets, and tennis balls.

I had saved some money from my newspaper experience in San Diego, so I had one of the few cars on campus. I remember Josephine Tone, who was a girl I liked. She wanted to go down to the drugstore off-campus to get some Kotex. So I drove her there, and coming back I said, "Can't you get that in the dorm?" She said "No." That answer gave me the idea to start selling Kotex at the bookstore. Then I started selling Kotex in the women's dorms. I just had a big box on the honor system. Soon I was making more money than any previous manager had made running the school store. I also made more money during my term than Wilcox, my co-op manager. I was in my element. I loved peddling! I was always watching for what might sell.

Being the co-manager of the bookstore was my work-study expcrience in my second year at Antioch. During that time, school officials told me that I should think about what other kind of work I would like to do, because a student could only be the manager of the bookstore for one year. Each year there would be a new pair of managers to give different students the experience. So I told them that I wanted to get a job with a public accounting firm. I had arrived at Antioch in the fall of 1929, so as my third year approached in 1931, we were deep into the Depression. The school officials said, "Mr. Colburn, we can't even place seniors in public accounting jobs. There just aren't any jobs. There are thousands of unemployed accountants, certified CPAs, walking the streets."

However, I had seen a couple of fellows several nights in succession in the school tearoom. We had a cafeteria where we regularly ate. But, if you bought a meal ticket for the semester, you could also eat in the tearoom. I had a little extra money, so I indulged myself. One evening, I introduced myself to these fellows and said that I had seen them around the campus for several days and wondered: "What were they there for?" They said they were auditing Antioch's books. They were with the Cleveland office of Lybrand, Ross Brothers & Montgomery. I said, "Gee, accounting is my major, and I want to work in public accounting. Would there possibly be an opening with your firm?" They said they didn't know, but they would talk to Mr.

Warren, who was the Cleveland manager. A week or so later, I got a letter from him telling me that they would like to hire me.

My first year of student employment was the 1929 to 1930 assignment at Westinghouse. My second year was 1930 to 1931 in the bookstore. Now I had an offer to work at Lybrand, Ross for my third year, which would be 1931 to 1932. I went into the extramural department, showed the personnel my letter, and said I had a job. They told Dean Henderson, who called me into his office and gave me hell. In response I said, "Why are you raising hell with me? The people to raise hell with are yourself and the extramural department. You never asked Lybrand, Ross for a student job. You are employing them to audit the school's books, and you don't even ask them if they have a spot for a student. You should commend me for getting my own job and making a future opportunity for the school and for other students." I really had a tangle with him. But despite that, everything ended well, and I worked for the accounting firm that third year.

During my fourth year of student employment, which was 1932 to 1933, the firm wanted to take another student along with me. The school submitted the résumés of two or three students, and the firm asked me whom I would recommend. I recommended Herb Stannard. The firm took Herb against the school's other recommendations. Again, I got hell from the college. By that time, Dean Henderson had replaced Morgan as president of Antioch, because Morgan had been appointed chairman of the Tennessee Valley Authority and had left the school. I said to Henderson, "Don't blame me if I recommended the better man. I think Herb is the best man for the job." Henderson said, "Who's to say who the better man is?" I replied, "Well, they asked me. Do you want me to lie?"

That argument was the first time I asked the question, "Do you want me to lie?" It's a conversation stopper: how can someone respond? Herb was asked back the next year, and he became manager of the office and a partner in the firm. In fact, he spent his life with that firm. So he must have been all right.

After my job at the Antioch bookstore, and while I still had the public accounting job, I made a proposal to manage the laundry, cleaning, and pressing needs of the student body. There had been a half-dozen fellow students coming through the dormitory offering laundry, dry cleaning, and pressing service. At a certain point, I got tired of having fellows come into my room to ask if I had any laundry to be done. I never had any laundry to go out, or any cleaning and pressing. The students pestering me represented laundries in Springfield, which was ten miles north of campus, and in Xenia, which was ten miles south of campus. These students came into the dormitories looking for business.

At that time, I was a kind of behind-the-scenes operator. I helped get my roommate elected president of the student body. Later, I presented a proposition to the student council to cut laundry, dry cleaning, and pressing costs. I said I would save them money, which I did, because of the large volume that I could achieve by having a monopoly. I pointed out that instead of six laundries coming to pick up laundry and deliver it, there could be one laundry and one dry cleaning-and-pressing agency. To achieve efficiencies, we introduced standard procedures. We didn't press any towels. We tumbled and folded towels. When an outside laundry, working under contract, would send down a pickup or delivery truck, it could pick up four times as much laundry or clothes for cleaning and pressing as before. I just put out a couple of tubs—canvas carts on wheels—for laundry, then put the laundry in a paper bag and put the student's name on it. The same procedure was done for dry cleaning, which was marked to be dry cleaned or pressed and then returned. I made some money from the laundry business while I was in school. When I was not at school, my friends ran the business for me. It only took one fellow to do what needed to be done. Money had to be collected from the students, but that was not difficult.

In my early business experiences, I learned to bargain tightly to control costs. I used to say to the managers, "Why don't you just take yourself off the payroll and work for the joy of working and for profit sharing?" I have been asked if it is part of my psychology in negotiating to make it look like I am offering something, even though I know they won't take the offer. Well, in profit sharing, I used to tell people, "The more you make, the more I make. To control your costs, take yourself off the payroll as an example to the rest of your colleagues. Get them all to work without a salary, but, through profit sharing, make even more money." Nobody ever took me up on my proposal.

I went to Antioch for four years. I had some credits from San Diego, so I didn't need the regular course of six years to finish. I had enough credits so that I would have received the degree in five years, concluding with the year starting in the fall of 1933. However, I would have had to stay at Antioch and take additional biology, geology, psychology, aesthetics, and philosophy courses to get my degree. But since this era was the middle of the Depression, I couldn't see taking those courses. I had learned enough to know that you don't learn anything in college that you can't teach yourself.

However, I also realized that there is a certain discipline in the academic life, as well as the competition and the stimulation of academic life. For geology, there would be the lectures, and then the class would walk up through Glen Helen—the equivalent of a wildlife preserve. The students would look at the plants, wildlife, turn over the rocks, and so forth. Geology sounded appealing. As for biology, I had started this course twice. I loved the lectures, but I hated the lab work in the afternoon because, if the weather was good, I preferred being out on the playing field. If the weather was not good, I wanted to be up in the attic playing bridge. I loved playing bridge.

I remember playing bridge one night in San Diego when I was home from Antioch for the summer. I used to go back to San Diego in the summer to play in the orchestra's program "Symphonies under the Stars." I also played bridge in San Diego. One memorable night that summer, my brother William and I played bridge out on a battleship in the San Diego Harbor. We were picked up at a dock and taken out to the ship. My brother and I played bridge all night with the executive officer and one of the other officers on the ship. I didn't like to play bridge for high stakes, so I would just get an hourly rate from my brother William for being his partner. I was a good bridge partner, but William took the risk. When I came home that morning, the milk wagon was delivering milk on the street. I was just in time for fresh milk.

My years at Antioch taught me a lot. I will never forget one particular girl I met. In those days at Antioch College, when you had only a week of holiday at Christmas and you were from California, you didn't have enough break time to travel home. It took three days to get out to California and three days to get back, so you just stayed at school. One Christmas this particular girl was on campus, and so was I. At that time, I was sleeping on the sleeping porch. During winter, most of the other fellows moved their beds off the sleeping porch and into a room. But I was still on the sleeping porch, with two heated slabs of limestone slate, about an inch thick, to keep me warm. I would leave them on the radiator in my room all day and then, at night, I would take them out and put them in the bed to warm it up before I got in bed. I don't know how it happened, but I do remember that I had taken my heated rocks out and put them in the bed, as I did every night. Then this girl and I went out and got into the bed. I was twenty-one, and I was so embarrassed by the experience that I never dated her again. I had a great sense of guilt. It took time to come to terms with what had happened.

I never graduated from Antioch. I didn't get a degree. But I had learned a little psychology, and I learned about aesthetics, including art and music. My mother had graduated from the Art Institute of Chicago, and I also learned a little about art from her. At that time I felt I knew more about music than my professors did. For many years I played violin in trios and viola in string quartets. When I was at Antioch, I played trios with Bill Lloyd, who later become a next door neighbor when we both lived in Winnetka.

I went back to San Diego the summer of 1933, as I had in the summers before. I played in "Symphonies under the Stars." I didn't go back to Antioch for my fifth year, since I didn't care about finishing the degree. Even today I don't feel that getting a college degree makes you any better a person than you would otherwise be. At the end of working at a job for that extra year, you might be worth more to an employer because of the work experience you've had. There are many different ways to learn, and there are many different skills that are useful to learn.

# CHAPTER 3

# Life after College

IN THE FALL OF 1933, I went back to Chicago to work for a public accounting firm, Allen R. Smart. It was a relatively small firm, but with top clients. I then got a job at Reliance in the garment industry to learn more about business. When I didn't see clear advancement at Reliance, I went to work for Booz Allen Hamilton, a consulting firm. After that job, I went out to California and worked for Columbia Steel, a U.S. Steel subsidiary. During these four jobs from late 1933 to fall 1942, I observed and learned some basic principles in business that stayed with me. I also married.

When I first came to Chicago, I lived with my cousin, Delmar Frye, at the Park Dearborn Hotel apartments on the North Side of Chicago. It was a one-room apartment with twin Murphy beds. Delmar and I used to go to Bloomington, Indiana, on weekends. The mother of the girl he was dating was a widow who owned quite a bit of wooded acreage of oak and hemlock trees. In the winter storms, a number of trees would fall down. On the weekend, Delmar and I would go out to the woods with a two-man cross cut saw, a mallet, and a couple of wedges. We would cut the tree trunks into appropriate lengths and split them with the wedges and the mallet, a hammer weighing about fifteen or twenty pounds with a three-foot-long handle. We would leave most of the split wood in the widow's basement, but would take some back to Chicago. After some time, Delmar left Chicago. He married his girlfriend and moved to Bloomington. As a result, I moved from the North Side to the South Side of Chicago, and lived with Bill Marburg. Bill was a younger brother of Nancy Marburg, who also had gone to Antioch and had married Fred Adams, a very good friend of mine there.

In Chicago, I met Dorothy Lane, who was called "America's most decorated harpsichordist." She was a student and colleague of Manuel and Williams. There was a resurgence of interest in Baroque music in the late 1930s and early 1940s. I almost married Dorothy, but then I met Elizabeth—and I ended up marrying her. I remember Dorothy coming and having lunch with me, trying to get things back on track. I just couldn't commit myself to Dorothy.

After rooming with Marburg, I got an apartment of my own, which was just a block from where I had been with him. I then decided I wanted to live at the International House on the University of Chicago campus. In order to be a resident at the International House, you had to be a student at the University of Chicago. So I took two courses at the university, one on the economics of imperfect competition and the other on statistics. At that time, I was working at Reliance in the garment business. I wanted to live at the International House because it seemed like an interesting social club. You met students from countries all over the world, and you ate and socialized with them. It had a good location, a handsome building, nice rooms, and pleasant people. I would never have met William Henry Krome

George, III had I not moved there. With Henry Savage, whom I knew from Antioch, we formed a kind of triumvirate at the International House.

After a certain point, however, the three of us were "invited" to move out, for reasons best forgotten. We moved off campus, across the Midway to an apartment at the Plaisance Hotel. There was daily maid service, as well as some other amenities. The three of us used to play field hockey out on the Midway. Every weekend, we'd drive east, around Lake Michigan, through Gary, to Indiana Dunes Park. They have a lot of sand dunes east of Gary on the south border, right on the lake. We'd walk the dunes, and then come back to Chicago.

During this time, Bill Cobb, a violist and one of my chamber-music-playing buddies, worked for an architectural firm in Chicago. I remember one weekend in Winnetka, a peaceful suburb north of Chicago, playing chamber music with him and Bill Lloyd, and another person whom I can't recall. Ruth Cobb told me they were going away on a six-month leave, and that they wanted somebody to rent their house. She asked me if I knew anybody who might like to rent it. I said, "Well, if you'd take three bachelors, I think we'd like to move in. I'll talk to my roommates." I talked to them, and they liked the idea, so we rented the house and the three of us moved out there. There was a part-time maid who took care of us. Six months passed. Bill and Ruth Cobb didn't return for a year and a half.

While I was still living in the International House, I would often see this cute, blue-eyed, red-headed girl in flat heels in line in the cafeteria at International House. Night after night, she always seemed to be alone, and she ate alone. I made some inquiries and found out what her name was. It was Elizabeth Whiting. I called her up one night and invited her to go out to dinner that night, and she turned me down. Then I called her again—I think two or three times—and was rejected. I asked if there was some reason why she wasn't willing at least to have a meal with me. She said something like, "Well, Mr. Colburn, you always call at the last minute. It makes me feel like I'm at the bottom of your list. If you asked me in advance, I think you would get a different response. But when you ask me at six o'clock to have dinner at seven-thirty, that doesn't sit well with me." I said, "Well, how about having dinner tomorrow night?" She said, "That's a date." So I had dinner with her the next night.

After that evening, I got to know her quite well. She worked with Rand McNally, the map publishing company, had graduated from the University of Illinois, and loved music. Her favorite opera was *The Magic Flute*; mine was *The Marriage of Figaro*. We agreed on Mozart, at least. Later when I had strep throat, she came out from Chicago to the house I was renting in Winnetka to see me. She went to Walgreens, got an ice pack for my throat, and brought it to me. While I lay in bed with strep throat, I thought about how all my friends had moved away and were getting married. Henry Savage had gotten a job in Liberia, West Africa, with Firestone Tire & Rubber. William Henry Krome George had taken a job in Baton Rouge, Louisiana with the Aluminum Company of America where they were building an aluminum smelter. I was living alone in the house. I wondered, "Well, now what am I going to do?" I thought of getting married. So, the first day that I had recovered from strep throat (and I hadn't even shaved for a week), I went down to her apartment. She shared it with another girl on the Near North Side of Chicago. She came out and we sat in the car. I asked her to marry me. She said, "Well, I would like to think about it." Soon, we were married.

Elizabeth and I first lived in the house in Winnetka that I was still renting from Cobb. When I later took a job in San Francisco as director of systems and procedures for Columbia Steel, we moved to a San Francisco apartment at the corner of Jackson and Laguna Streets. In time, we had three blue-eyed, red-headed children. Richard Whiting Colburn was born in San Francisco. Carol Dunton Colburn was born in Evanston, Illinois. Keith Whiting Colburn was also born in Evanston, not far from Winnetka, where we lived at the time.

# CHAPTER 4

# Learning about Business

~

THE PUBLIC ACCOUNTING FIRM, ALLEN R. Smart, with which I went to work in the fall of 1933, has since been "merged out of existence." I worked on the audits of many of its top-grade clients, including the Kroger Company, Valvoline Oil, Mead Paper Company, Curtiss-Wright, and United Aircraft, a large conglomerate. United Aircraft was forced, due to legislation during the Roosevelt Administration, to break up and divest itself of Hamilton Standard Propeller, Pratt & Whitney, Sikorsky Aircraft, Boeing Aircraft, Western Airlines, and United Airlines because it made propellers, engines, and aircraft, and owned two airlines. For the accounting work I was doing at that time one didn't need to be a certified public accountant. I saw and learned about industry—and of the spectacular successes of some individuals in industry. For example, Charles F. Kettering had invented the automobile starter and became one of the largest General Motors shareholders. I knew that a fellow by the family name of Patterson was the president of National Cash Register, and he had built that company from nothing.

At Allen R. Smart, I quickly learned that wealth-accumulating possibilities in public accounting were very limited.

All one was doing was selling time, and there's a limit to how much one can sell one's time. So, in 1935, I decided to leave Allen R. Smart and find employment in industry, which I think was the best decision that I could have made.

I went to work for Reliance Manufacturing Company, which was headquartered on Monroe Street in Chicago. Reliance was in the "rag business"—a manufacturer of work clothing and other low-priced garments, primarily for men. I was hired at Reliance as an accountant, but in about two years was promoted to office manager. I then had responsibility for about 110 employees who were working on order entry, accounts payable, accounts receivable, payroll, general ledger, and facilities supervision.

At Reliance, I made a point of being the first in the office in the morning and the last out at night. I think that without consciously articulating it, I intuitively drew from my earlier experience and observations at Westinghouse. I wanted to be first in and last out. This commitment made an impression. Senior managers noticed that I was almost always there when they arrived in the morning, and that I was almost always there when they left at night. So, when the time came for them to choose an office manager, they selected me.

When I started as the office manager, almost everyone working in the office was older than I was, except for a few women in the filing department. I had a secretary who was thirty-four years old. So there I was, this young "whippersnapper," supervising many employees who were old enough to be my father or mother. As the office manager, I made many changes. These changes resulted in a state of uninterrupted confusion in certain areas. Since it is in human nature to resist change,

I had the continuing problem, or challenge, of needing to be persuasive.

I joined Reliance soon after the implementation of five important federal laws that had a significant impact upon Reliance. The first law was the federal prohibition of interstate commerce in prison-made products. Reliance had been manufacturing clothing using prisoners within eighteen state prisons in the South and Midwest. When I joined Reliance, the company had just completed the relocation of these plants from prisons into vacant manufacturing facilities in the communities in which the prisons were located. This involved moving cutting tables, sewing machines, and raw materials and finished-product storage. In Kokomo, Indiana, Reliance moved into the former Auburn Cord automobile plant. Reliance had a factory in Anamosa, Iowa, totally dedicated to making work shirts for J. C. Penney. I also remember Reliance had factories in Loogootee, Indiana, and in Hattiesburg, Mississippi. Reliance had to pay rent and maintain buildings, whereas previously, of course, Reliance didn't have to maintain the prisons.

The second law was the passage of the Fair Labor Standards Act. This legislation set the minimum wage for an eight-hour day with time-and-a-half for work over eight hours in a day, or for a sixth day of work in a week, and double time for the seventh day. At that time, Reliance was paying ten cents an hour for women at the sewing machines that had previously been operated for little or nothing by prison inmates. When Reliance had prison labor, about the only significant costs were the contributions paid to politicians to get the plants into the prisons.

The third law was legislation initiating the crop-support program. This bill raised the price of cotton from five cents a pound to twenty cents a pound, quadrupling the price of raw materials from which virtually all of Reliance's garments were produced. The piece goods from which the garments were made had previously been dirt-cheap with cotton at five cents a pound. The increase in labor and material costs dramatically increased the selling prices needed to cover these increased costs.

The fourth was tax legislation in conjunction with the crop-support program. The legislation imposed a so-called floor tax on the cotton content of products in the inventory of every user of cotton in the supply chain. The government set up the "floor tax" to equalize the burden of the crop support program on the inventory of everyone using raw materials affected by the crop-support program. So, the taxes Reliance had to pay on the cotton content of its work-in-process and finished goods went up substantially. At the same time that this "floor-tax" program was initiated, another tax was imposed on the inventories in order to more evenly distribute the impact of the increased raw material cost arising from this program.

When the crop-support legislation was introduced, it generated enormous inequities all the way through the system. For example, the fortunate farmers were those who still had their recent crops in their own barns, compared to those farmers who had already sold their crops for five cents a pound instead of the new price of twenty cents a pound. Therefore, at every level, there were inequities that required a business to either pay a tax or file a claim with the government. I had the responsibility both for clarifying that inequity for Reliance and for filing our claims. I remember going to Washington with Richard Meyer, one of the partners of Mayer, Meyer, Austin & Platt, our lawyers in Chicago. Richard's brother Herbert was the president of Reliance. Reliance had an income tax issue, and I did a good job of settling this tax issue with the government. I think I was twenty-six years old at the time, so it would have been 1937.

The fifth area of legislation involved payroll taxes. Reliance's costs were increased substantially by the imposition of a payroll tax in support of the unemployment compensation program. Company costs were increased further by a payroll tax for the support of the Social Security program.

All of these legislative changes drastically increased the costs of Reliance's products. At that point Reliance needed to know much more about its costs than it previously had to know. Raw material costs were dramatically increasing, and Reliance no longer had prison labor. Now Reliance had to meet a much higher payroll, and it took a lot more money to run the business. Reliance had to pay over four times as much for its raw materials, in part because labor costs for the cloth weavers went up, just as Reliance's own labor costs went up. Reliance now had to borrow money from the banks to carry a larger, higher-cost inventory and to finance increased labor costs throughout the organization.

A new learning experience then began for me—borrowing money from the Continental Illinois National Bank, which was on the first floor of the building in which Barcus, Kindred and the law firm of Mayer, Meyer, Austin & Platt were located. I was heavily involved with the bank discussions because I was best-informed about the fluctuating cash needs of the company. Reliance ended up with a line of credit that permitted easy borrowing and repayment of money with interest rates geared to the prime rate. I was quick to learn from this borrowing experience.

I remember that later a Bank of America advertisement stated, "We rent money." In effect, Reliance was re-renting money that had been rented to a bank by its depositors, who were paid a lower rental or interest rate. The bank then re-rented their depositors' money at a much higher interest rate to Reliance.

To enable Reliance's sewing machine operators to earn more money per hour than their base rate, and to identify those women whose productivity did not support the payment to them of their base hourly rate, a standard-allowed-hour was established by time studies for performance of each sewing operation on each product. If a woman produced less than the standard output for the number of hours spent at her machine, then she needed to bring her output up to standard or she would be replaced.

The "manufacturing people" were responsible for defining the sewing operations required. But I did have to know what different things were needed—like buttons and thread—and I had to understand the required procedures. A time study established how long each stitching operation should take. One woman did nothing but make buttonholes, and another woman did nothing but stitch on buttons. Another woman put collars onto shirts. The garment business is still regarded as simple and straight-forward. Hand-operated machines, following the borders of the patterns, cut the multiple layers of cloth. The sewing was easy to learn. All of these operations in sequence were recorded on what we called "the bundle ticket," which was a method of tracking time and productivity. When each sewing process was completed, the worker clipped off the bottom of the bundle ticket showing the operation and the standard allotted hours and placed it on her time card. Then

the bundle ticket (along with the garments being stitched together) was passed to the next worker in sequence for the next
operation on the bundle ticket.

In the order department, women manually tabulated the
orders by product identification, size, waist measurement, the
inseam, sleeve length, or other specifics related to the garment
being produced. Initially, Reliance really hadn't had much direct cost. The biggest cost related to the contract to operate at
the prison facilities and to adapt the facilities to the needs of
the garment manufacturing processes, such as storage of finished goods and shipping. But with rising costs due to the new
legislation, the company needed to develop a system to moni-
tor costs, and that was my responsibility. Inventory control was
also my responsibility. To accomplish inventory control, we tabulated the collar sizes and sleeve lengths on shirts, inseams and
waists on pants, and so on, and it became quite a costly clerical
job to tabulate all of this manually.

As a result, I started investigating both IBM and Remington
Rand systems for automating our tabulation. They both had
punch-card systems. Remington Rand had round holes in the
cards, and IBM had rectangular holes in the cards. Remington
Rand had pins that went up through the holes, and IBM had
electrical contacts. I decided upon an IBM installation. I developed the new system in collaboration with the IBM systems-
design personnel. Under the system we designed, when each
woman performed an operation, she'd slit or cut off the card
section for the operation she had performed and paste it onto
her own time card. I remember explaining to management
how this all worked—the new principle of paying people for
what they produced rather than for the time they spent on the
job.

The company had a tub of cards that were for unfilled orders. Each item and every order was translated onto a punch card that went into a tub of unfilled orders sequenced by shipping date. The quantities, various sizes, sleeve lengths, etcetera, were all captured on the punch cards. The women would sit and punch these cards, with each item on an order resulting in a separate card. From those cards we knew how many hours it took—total allowed-hours we called them—to make a shirt or to do different tasks. As a result, Reliance could quickly adjust delivery dates as it sold out its manufacturing capacity. Or, if Reliance was getting short of some material, the company either had to withdraw an item from the product line or purchase additional material to continue to manufacture the product line.

With this new system, an alert plant manager could flick through the cards at the end of the day to see who was producing in accordance with the standard-allotted-hours system. The plant manager could identify the slow producers and ask these women politely, "What is your problem, dear? So-and-so did ten hours of work yesterday and you only did six. What happened, dear? What can we do to help?" Along with the paycheck for the personnel at each plant, the manager received a payroll summary by employee showing the number of hours worked, number of standard-allotted-hours of work produced, and the amount of the gross paycheck. Later on, as payroll deductions were mandated, they were shown together with the net payment per check. With this new detail, the plant manager could more quickly identify those employees not producing as much work as they were being paid for, and then had the responsibility of addressing those poor producers.

Another idea I had as office manager concerned efficiencies in the central stenographic pool. We used Dictaphones with round cylinders. I started requesting a count each day of the cylinders that each girl transcribed. If one person was lagging behind others, I would ask her what her problem was, why couldn't she transcribe as many letters as other secretaries could transcribe.

One Saturday, I had one of my colleagues come in with me and we went through every desk in the office. You wouldn't believe what we found! We found orders, checks, stockings, condoms, shoes, and garter belts. You name it, everything imaginable was in the desks. I decided that I wanted to get rid of all the desks and have only tables, but that was too expensive. Instead, I just got an in-box and out-box for every desk, and mandated that nothing was to go into a drawer. What came in, one had to get rid of; paper had to go from the in-basket to the out-basket. Through this process, one always had to do something with that piece of paper. If we found anything in a drawer, in anybody's drawer: "goodbye." Reliance had a central filing system so people didn't need personal files.

An in-box and out-box was a new idea in that office, but I had seen the boxes elsewhere. At Reliance there was a tray on the left and a tray on the right of the desk. But if you go in my office now, the tray has two decks; papers come in the upper level and go out the lower level. If a paper comes to me, it either goes into the wastebasket, the out-basket for filing after I have read it, or into a pile for correspondence, which is sitting on top of my desk. Actually, although I say desk, I sit at a table. I always sit at a table, one without drawers. I don't believe in drawers.

I remember another innovation at Reliance that I thought was important. We had duplicate-copy pads made with the statement, "Write it. Don't say it." These pads proved necessary because I had so many discussions that ended with my being told, "No, I didn't say this. No, I didn't say that." Soon I was prepared. When I heard these statements of denial I would just go and get my little pad and show them my copy. Even to this day, if I have an important conversation, I will immediately write a memo confirming our discussion. I learned long ago that what I thought I said was not always what other people thought they heard. So I would write, "If this is not in accord with your understanding of what we agreed, please drop me a note." It takes time to write these memos, but they pay off by reducing misunderstandings.

At some point I read Dale Carnegie's book, *How to Win Friends and Influence People.* One of the recommendations made in the book stayed with me: "Be lavish in praise and sparing in criticism." The suggestion was useful when I became the manager of the office at Reliance. It was a critical period of economic changes for the company. With the increased cost for us of labor, materials, and plant maintenance, we had to develop systems for reducing costs. One cost-saving approach that we developed was making pants in one seam-length. It was cheaper to just make one length and then cut off and throw away the extra leg length than it was to put cuffs on the pants at various lengths. This innovation changed the entire manufacturing procedure. I remember going over the consequences of this change with the merchandise managers, showing them how the recent wage and materials price increases affected us and how the new pant-cuff procedure worked. I was a "pipsqueak" explaining what we needed to do to the senior managers who earned high salaries. (I knew what everybody was paid because I did the payroll.) It could be said that I was a young kid telling the old-timers "how the cows eat the cabbage." In an effort to ease tension, I practiced the maxim, "Be lavish in praise and sparing in criticism."

When the war came along, William Henry Krome George, Henry Savage, and I went to apply for commissions as ensigns in the Navy. You could take certain tests, and if you were accepted, you got a pretty good assignment. You weren't just toting a gun. George was rejected on general health reasons, and Savage was rejected because of poor eyesight. At that time, I was running the office at Reliance. We were making clothing for the Army and Navy, and we made parachutes that just involved stitching pieces of cloth together. I don't think we used any silk at all; the material might have been nylon. So they gave me a critical job deferment, a 2A classification. They rejected me. They said, "All we'd be doing with you, Mr. Colburn, is moving you from one desk to another. I don't think that the government would benefit. Reliance would have to train someone to take your place, and we would have to train you. So we're just going to leave you where you are." Hence, I spent part of the war years running that office at Reliance.

While I was at Reliance, the merchandising department received instructions to change the products to war materials, particularly military shorts and parachutes for the Army and Navy. So Reliance started making parachutes. A parachute is just pieces, or panels, stitched up and packed. The packing is very important. If you don't pack the parachute right, it doesn't open right and the jumper may go plunging to the ground. I didn't have anything to do with this conversion to war materials in the manufacturing at Reliance. The business was organized around merchandising, manufacturing, and paper processing, as in most businesses. I was not involved in marketing, sales, product design, or manufacturing at Reliance. I was exclusively involved in the "paper processing" (PP), which requires patience and perseverance (PP).

By late 1941, I became increasingly aware that there were no new worlds to conquer at Reliance, and the only promotion I was interested in was the presidency, which was obviously beyond my reach for at least ten years under the most favorable circumstances. It seemed to me at the time that the best next step for me to take was to seek an association with Booz Allen Hamilton. That firm was then in the early years of its growth into a world-wide management consulting practice. It had done some work for Reliance. During the firm's work with Reliance, I had some contact with Edwin Booz, founder of the firm, who suggested to me that if I thought of leaving Reliance, I might consider joining him. I remember him telling me, "In the rag business, you are guided by the feel of the cloth. In our consulting business, the feel of the man guides us. You work with the design of the pattern and the cutting and stitching of the cloth. I work with the design of an organization and with the fitting of men." He captured the similarities between what he was doing for Reliance as a consultant and what we did at Reliance in our work.

I remember who interviewed and hired me at Booz Allen Hamilton—G. Carson Ellis. He was smooth and polished. He must have been the personnel officer of the firm. I also was tested for Booz Allen Hamilton by an evaluation firm, and the test included both written and oral sections. Booz Allen Hamilton tested new employees by exploring their aptitude for service and other kinds of issues. The tests were also used for determining appropriate salary levels. As a result, Booz Allen Hamilton got a detailed perception of the person they were considering. The testing process fascinated me. And I must have "tested well" because I did receive a good offer.

Thus in 1942, I joined Booz Allen Hamilton, which had its headquarters in Chicago. I worked on two consulting assignments that entailed developing compensation programs, first for a major law firm, and then for a large medical practice partnership, which was operating a hospital.

The question on the medical practice assignment was how to split up the financial "pot," the total take of the practice. Resolving questions of compensation can be complicated. It's not possible to please every member of a group. I never knew a fellow who would say, "I don't need anything more. I married a Rockefeller, and she has more money than we could ever spend in ten lifetimes." I think people would never express an indifference to their income, or believe that income should just be divided equally. Surgeons, because of the nature of their work and the market, are able to bill way more money for their work than other doctors. Similarly with law firms, the big fees generally go to the litigators, not to the lawyers who draft contracts and draw wills. There was a case recently in which the judge allowed over $300 million in legal fees to go to about twelve law firms. How does each law firm split up its share of that fee? How do the firms agree how much each firm will get? These are often difficult issues.

To help determine what to recommend on splitting the doctors' pot, I talked to all doctors privately to gain their thoughts on how they would do it and why, what was wrong with their current approach, and who would administer the plan. This issue was inherently complicated for a group medical practice. When patients come in they are often assigned to a general practitioner for a thorough evaluation, depending on their symptoms. The patients may then see an ophthalmologist or an urologist or a proctologist, and so on. The doctors may end up deciding that the patient has a growth on his left lung and it's cancerous. The next step is deciding what they are going to do about the cancer. Are they going to operate? Are they going to offer chemotherapy? Are they going to use radiation?

The medical practice shouldn't let money influence the decision. But in a complicated medical case, several different doctors could think that they should have medical control of the patient. At this point, one has to take the motivation of money out of consideration as much as possible to get people to think collectively about optimizing patient care. The same situation often exists in a legal practice. Do we sue the opponents, do we negotiate, or do we go into mediation? Do we try to arbitrate? Should it be compulsory or noncompulsory arbitration? Do we leave the door open for litigation, or do we do all that is possible to avoid litigation? The resolution of these questions shapes the economics of the law firm and the "profit centers" it may comprise.

Another key question for a medical practice or for a law firm is how much does the headquarters staff get paid, compared with the compensation going to people working in the profit centers? Should the people at headquarters—the staff who do the billing, collect the money, pay the bills, vacuum the rugs, wash the windows, file the tax returns, and so forth—share in the returns that the profit centers generate? In some respects, those at headquarters are the hired hands; they are the servants of the profit centers. In some situations, that's what I tend to suggest to the headquarters people: they live to serve the profit-center people. But you also should be trying to motivate all of the people and keep them working together with a reasonable degree of harmony and cooperation. If you extend the profit-sharing plan to the sweeper in the headquarters, everybody has a sense of common identity of interests. That's what one should usually be trying to build, an identity of interests. How do you best serve the interests of the total group of which you are a member?

One of the issues faced by consultants on such compensation plan assignments was what to do with the older partner who's near retirement? Does the firm set aside income to provide retirement for members who stop work because of age or disability? Does the firm have, or should it establish, a compulsory retirement age? How does the partnership set this retirement income? How do we compensate senior people who have clients or patients continually coming back to them because people tend to go to the doctor or lawyer they know? How should compensation plans reflect the fact that some primary care physicians need counsel from the rest of their teammates who are specialists? The same issues arise in law practices.

The compensation plan assignments required us to be sensitive to human relationships. When interviewing a new client, one of the first questions I would ask was, "If you were in my place, what would you do?" Sometimes I would say, "My firm has been hired to review the compensation arrangements for you and your colleagues. To start with, we can both probably agree there is no perfect answer. From your vantage point of having been here for ten years, what would you do to the current system if you were to change it at all?" I would ask them, "How do you fit into the scheme of things? Do you think your role should be changed, and, if so, how?" I found this approach to working with clients to be helpful. Later, when I had my own businesses and was a great user of profit sharing, we would ask the same question, "How do you divide the profits?" It is always a key question.

Both of those compensation-consulting assignments were conducted at locations hundreds of miles away from the Chicago area. I would leave my home and family late Sunday night or early Monday morning, and I would return home late Friday night or Saturday morning. Therefore, after being with Booz Allen Hamilton for about six months, I decided that I wanted different working conditions. So I went to an employment agency. Through this agency, I quickly obtained a position as director of systems and procedures with Columbia Steel in California. Mr. Fields, a newly appointed systems and procedures director for the parent company, U.S. Steel, hired me. Columbia Steel was headquartered in San Francisco and had three operating steel mills in the United States. Columbia Steel moved my wife Elizabeth and me to San Francisco. This move took me back close to my earlier life in San Diego.

Before starting my Columbia Steel assignment, I spent about six weeks of orientation in and around Pittsburgh, Pennsylvania, where I visited coal and limestone mines, mills with their coke-plant blast furnaces, and rolling mills. This place was the first time I ever saw men sitting on stools with green eyeshades and black sleeve-protectors, protecting their long shirtsleeves from the dust while involved in "paper processing." U.S. Steel was so antiquated compared with what I had been doing at Reliance. I thought to myself, "These people are still in the Middle Ages!"

Upon my arrival in California, I met Columbia Steel's president and the senior staff with whom I would be working. One of my main responsibilities was to find ways to simplify the paper processing and to eliminate unneeded personnel by changing to more modern paper-processing systems and procedures. This task is never easy because people, quite understandably, resist change. But one must recognize that change is inevitable. Columbia Steel was, oddly enough, losing money at a time when the war effort could use every ton of steel that could be produced in the country. Columbia Steel had the only mills within the U.S. Steel parent company that were losing money. What was the problem? Clearly Columbia Steel was poorly managed, and because of price controls on Columbia Steel's output, there was a need for cost reduction. Productivity of the workforce needed to be increased. Management, therefore, created my new position, but I don't think they knew what else they were going to do themselves, except they knew they were in trouble.

Firing the president wasn't going to solve the problem. My task, instead, was to find more economical ways of conducting every aspect of the steel business. That's what business is all about: to sell more for more, produce it for less, and reduce expenses. Understandably, the Columbia Steel organization was uneasy about possible changes in "systems and procedures." People initially thought of me as "a hatchet man," but they knew that my job was to find ways to cut costs at every level. Still, they thought they were doing their jobs well and didn't want anybody meddling—someone coming in and saying, "get rid of this person, do this, and do that." They were worried that my attention in their areas would imply that a person was not getting the job done as well as necessary—or that they didn't have the courage to make the changes on their own initiative. Sometimes I would be told, "Yes, I know. Dick, you're right. I should have done it." What most impressed me in my work with Columbia Steel was how protective individuals are of their little domains, and the length individuals will go to protect their fiefdoms. In contrast to my prior experiences at Reliance, I encountered a great deal of resistance at Columbia Steel to implementing new organizational systems and procedures. I learned that there is rarely universal agreement on change.

I was on the job at Columbia Steel less than six months when I was offered a position with Barcus, Kindred, a Chicago-headquartered firm that had significant capital in excess of the needs of its bond business and which was searching for someone to help redeploy excess capital. Barcus, Kindred offered to double my salary and give me an eight percent carried interest, at four percent accrued interest per annum on any acquisition I could persuade them to make. I could not refuse this offer. Once I made that decision, it took me a couple of months to extricate myself from Columbia Steel. My wife and I had moved out to San Francisco by train, shipping out our car, and my oldest son Richard was born in San Francisco. However, we turned around and went right back to Illinois. Richard, our baby, was only eight or nine months old. He rode in the back seat of the car in a cardboard grocery box.

As I reflect on these early work experiences, I think they helped me develop a way of managing and of doing business that provided the following key lessons that helped me later in life.

My first important lesson from this period is the importance of providing service. One has to do a good job and give good service. This lesson goes back to my newspaper days.

The second lesson is that sales make a business. Sales make jobs. If a business can't create demand for its product or service, no matter what it is, the business will fail. Going back to the newspaper boy experience, initially the newspaper boy paid his price for the papers and then he got his payment later from the customer. He had the risk of bad debts and had the cost of the collection procedures. So sales are essential. Demand for a product generates income. Selling opens up one's opportunities.

The third lesson I learned is that, irrespective of the size of the business, a business is all about people. One has to get people to work together toward a common goal with the least amount of conflict or misunderstanding, and with a reasonable degree of peace and tranquility. In fact, one of the most important decisions in any business is the choice of the people to whom to delegate.

The fourth lesson is profit sharing. I saw that a significant way to motivate people to work toward a common goal was with profit sharing. I saw this with the newspaper boys. As they increased their circulation, they increased their own profit, as well as mine. Later in labor bargaining, I would say, "Make more for me and you'll make more money for yourself." Profit sharing can create a common goal.

The fifth lesson I learned is to set examples by the quality of one's own leadership, working particular hours and clearly being "first in and last out." One did not necessarily need to work long hours. You could arrive before others and stay five minutes longer than everyone else. But it is important to show commitment. "Early and late" hours also help one keep a finger on the pulse of the employees. At Westinghouse, I saw a tremendous waste of human resources because of the perceived weak commitment of the president, who came in late and left early.

The sixth lesson I learned is always to look for new opportunities. As manager of the Antioch bookstore I learned to look for new products and to broaden the scope of products offered to fit demand.

The seventh lesson is to bargain tightly to control investment and operating costs. A related principle, "Buy right. The profit is in the purchase," falls into this category of bargaining tightly to control costs. By managing investment costs as well as operating expenses, one doesn't dissipate one's potential operating profit. Control one's expenses by imposing efficiency. Establish some standard of performance and hold people's feet to the fire. My first such experience was with those six or eight women transcribing cylinders in the central stenographic pool at Reliance, transcribing every letter that came out of the manufacturing offices or the merchandising offices. Some women met the standard of performance and some didn't. Adequate efficiency must be the standard of performance.

The eighth lesson I learned is the value and importance of building tangible things in industry. I learned this lesson at my first accounting job with Allen R. Smart. I have observed how when one looks around one sees homes, schools, hospitals, churches, paved streets, street lights, grocery stores, clothing stores, all kinds of other stores, skyscrapers, and so forth. All of these buildings represent the cumulative result of production in excess of consumption. In other words, there must be savings. Savings make investment possible. The lesson for each of us—and for society at large—is to produce more goods and services than we consume.

The ninth lesson is to be sure one knows what people mean when they say something. When someone says "we," I want to know who "we" are. And "there"—I don't know where "there" is. Is it heaven or hell or someplace else? I want people to be clear so that I know what is being considered. I like precision. At Reliance I saw how written memos emphasizing precision could reduce the disputes about who said what when. "Write it. Don't say it!"

The tenth lesson is to develop a personal sense of entrepreneurialism. Selling one's time limits one's income. In contrast, selling one's productivity puts no upper limit on one's income.

The eleventh lesson is the concept of authority withheld. Determine what degree of authority one really has when a project is started because one cannot do something without team effort and management support. At Columbia Steel I saw that I should have determined the degree of authority I had before I started the job. When one starts a job or project, it is important to find out what limits there are on one's authority. For example, it is critical to know if one cannot hire or fire, or change the compensation or the scope of an immediate subordinate's job without the concurrence of higher authority.

The twelfth lesson is: the bigger the business, the bigger the paper flow. This lesson I learned at Columbia Steel. In big business, the problems are bigger in size and scope but similar in type to the problems confronting small businesses. The simplest comparison is the legal office. The one-lawyer office may practice all kinds of law: tax law, inheritance law, real-estate law, criminal law, probates of wills and trusts, and so forth. However, in the larger law firms in the United States, these areas are usually divided. The firm will have a department that deals mostly with matters relating to the Securities and Exchange Commission, and other departments that deal with labor contracts, estate planning, or real estate transactions. Typically, a law firm will not take a new law case from a person if there is any possible conflict of interest with other clients. As a result, in a large firm they have to circulate a note to every department to see if there has been a prior relationship with this party or this firm. If a firm has only one man who does everything, one just has to talk with that one fellow. I call someone up at a large law firm and ask him about this or that, and he says, "Well, Dick, I don't think we have any conflict, but I'll have to circulate a note to my partners to see if that is the case." Consultation takes time. Everything is more complex because more people get involved in the decision process.

The thirteenth lesson concerns how to accomplish things. I am usually "behind-the-scenes." This role might be key to understanding how I work. In my earlier career, because of limits to my authority, I usually didn't have the ability to do everything I wanted. Maybe that constraint taught me that sometimes it is better to do what needs to be done as quietly as possible. A good example is how the important business of a board of directors is often done outside the boardroom on an individual basis in private face-to-face meetings. With any controversial issue, one person is going to have one attitude and another person is going to have a different attitude. Thus, a decision is best made quietly and in advance. Reach concurrence, if possible, outside the boardroom.

The fourteenth lesson is that labor unions tend to support the inefficient worker. I'm opposed to labor unions because they protect the indolent. Good people don't need the protection of a union.

The fifteenth, and concluding, lesson is that regulation either drives problems out of sight or places them in the inefficient and disruptive arbitration-negotiation territory of the courts. When regulation drives problems out of sight, those problems don't generally get the visibility needed to be quickly treated and resolved.

In joining Barcus, Kindred, I not only doubled my salary but also had the direct line responsibility for the management of each acquisition. With Barcus, Kindred, I moved from the role of the employed to the role of an executive officer. It was a dramatic change.

CHAPTER 5

# Management

DURING 1943, KEITH KINDRED TRACKED me down in San Francisco while I was working at Columbia Steel. Kindred had heard about me from two of my Reliance contacts, Russ Zimmerman, a Price Waterhouse partner who was Reliance's auditor, and Richard Meyer, who had been repeatedly referred to me by his brother Herbert, president of Reliance. Richard Meyer was a partner in the law firm of Mayer, Meyer, Austin & Platt with whom I had gone to Washington some years earlier on Reliance's behalf.

Keith Kindred identified himself as being a partner in the tax-exempt bond firm of Barcus, Kindred. He said he would like to come out to San Francisco and visit with me. I didn't have anything to lose but my time, which he said would be well spent. I gave my consent, and he came out to San Francisco. We had lunch together at the Mark Hopkins Hotel.

Barcus, Kindred was an underwriter and distributor of tax-exempt general obligation and revenue bonds issued by such governmental entities as cities, counties, and states to finance such special-purpose projects as libraries, fire stations, toll ways, subways, and facilitates for irrigation, sewer, and electrical power generation and distribution.

Two things were happening to financial markets during the war: the volume of underwriting by bond dealers had decreased and the easy availability of loans had made capital cheap. During the war, cities had a declining ability to build libraries, fire stations and schools, lay sewer lines, or do many other things for which municipal bonds are normally issued. Cities couldn't do many of these projects because they would have required a diversion of war resources for non-essential purposes. When a city wants to do something like build a library or school or lay a sewer line, it often sells bonds. Dealers bid for the bonds and then they sell them to investors. In some states, negotiated contracts to purchase the bonds are permitted. In some of those locations you don't have to admit that you have a friend in government or that you are somebody's aunt, or are pals with a city councilman, or whatever. A dealer purchases the bonds and resells them to insurance companies, banks, pension plans, and individuals. But, because the bond businesses contracted during the war, bond dealers such as Kindred and his partners had more capital than they could profitably employ.

Kindred and his partners, Jim Barcus and Jim Tucker, had a lot of capital unemployed and they were looking for ways to put it to work. Kindred told me they were looking for somebody to help them get into other investments. They had asked around the Chicago business community to get suggestions for some young fellow they might employ to get them into other kinds of businesses. I remember Kindred telling me at lunch that when he made inquiries mine was a name that was repeated.

Kindred offered to double the salary I was getting, to reimburse my expenses in moving back to Chicago, and to give me an eight percent carried interest in any business I was able to persuade Barcus, Kindred to buy. The interest rate I had to pay was four percent per annum. A "carried" interest means that if the partners bought a business for $1 million, my share of that investment and cost would be $80,000. If they were to put up the $80,000 for me, they would charge me four percent interest on that amount. So, if the business were to earn ten percent on the $1 million investment, I would have made six percent on $80,000 effectively. If the business were to be sold, I would get eight percent of the profits, less the cost of the four percent compounded interest on the money put up for me. Barcus, Kindred just wanted to employ its capital, and that is basically what the partners wanted me to do. They believed that giving me that carried interest would be an incentive. To be sure, they would get the best end of any deal, but they had to put up all the money. I couldn't refuse this offer.

President Roosevelt had persuaded Congress in 1935 to pass the Public Utility Holding Company Act, which required public utilities to divest themselves of what were described as non-integrated properties. For example, if a utility that served the Dallas-Fort Worth area also owned a little power plant in Arizona that was not integrated into the Dallas system, this Arizona plant wasn't part of their system. The purpose of the act was to encourage the development of integrated systems. Because Barcus, Kindred had been involved in the financing of some municipal power plant extensions, it was aware of the requirement for disposal of non-integrated properties. Barcus, Kindred thought this presented an opportunity. So, my first assignment in 1943 was to see if I could buy, on favorable terms, any independent "cat and dog" utilities or non-integrated parts of larger companies.

There were many little non-integrated utilities all over the country. On behalf of Barcus, Kindred, the Arizona Power Company (TAPCO) was established to purchase three small utilities in northern Arizona: one each in Flagstaff, Winslow, and Prescott. TAPCO built interconnecting lines for these small utilities along the Santa Fe Railroad line from Holbrook on the east to Seligman on the west. Then TAPCO built an interconnection with a line going down through Oak Creek Canyon and over Mingus Mountain to Prescott. TAPCO also had an interconnection with the public utility named Central Arizona Light and Power Company (CALAPCO), which served the Salt River Valley in which Phoenix was the dominant community. The part of northern Arizona TAPCO served included some Indian reservations. As a result, there would be electrical cords coming down from the center of many hogans, the little round structures in which the Indians lived.

When buying these utilities, I realized that buying "right" didn't necessarily refer only to the price paid. Consideration also had to be given to the condition of the company and its potential for profit. When trying to buy right, I always wanted to be sure that one could eventually get out of any investment with a profit of at least one dollar. During my twenty-year association with Barcus, Kindred, I enjoyed the counsel—when making purchases—of Leonard Spacek, a good friend of Kindred's and a man of exceptional judgment and wisdom. Spacek, the managing partner of Arthur Andersen, then headquartered in Chicago, directly succeeded Arthur Andersen, founder of the firm.

When we brought the three Arizona utilities together in one system, the only significant operating cost we encountered was the cost of generating power. With its new well-integrated system, TAPCO no longer needed the Winslow plant. But a utility should always have reserve power, which requires having a generator. Since it takes time to get a generator up to speed, one always wants to have a back-up generator turning. Then, if there were a sudden surge in demand, the company could bring the level of power output up quickly. Once TAPCO had its units interconnected, TAPCO didn't need to have separate backups for each plant. TAPCO also had some hydroelectric power, which is the cheapest electric power available. And TAPCO had the benefit of a power interchange agreement with CALAPCO through the interconnection of their two systems in Wickenburg.

As this utility system came into being, I could see right away that there were significant cost-saving opportunities, and we took steps to get the benefit of them. I saw there would be the potential advantage of having one office instead of three offices: one office rent to pay, one switchboard operator to pay, and one set of stationery to buy. TAPCO kept the best employees of the three companies, but we now didn't need three superintendents. There also were efficiencies available in the procedures for construction that couldn't be realized individually in the smaller utilities. In many areas TAPCO could affect operational savings.

The Prescott unit had two hydroelectric plants located on federal land and powered by an uninterrupted flow of water that came out of the mountains at a height between 4,000 and 5,000 feet. The water flowed down a precipitous drop from that height to the lower level of our Pelton wheel. This hydroelectric power satisfied our base-load of demand. If we didn't have any other needs, which we always had, we could just use that hydroelectric plant. This power was basically free. TAPCO only had to spend a little money to maintain the flume by having a man walk the flume every day to spot leakages needing repair, avoiding the loss of water while it flowed from the spring to the first precipitous drop. We had a dam below the first fall where we could store water and then release it when needed for the next power generation.

We were in competition with the Rural Electrification Administration (REA). It had first priority on federal-output-generated power, such as from the Hoover Dam. The REA had first preference to carry other people's electricity to supply rural community needs. As a result TAPCO would have competition in its territory if REA became active in the area. Therefore, we were motivated in Arizona to be involved with community elections and to discourage officials from voting to start an REA project.

In the meantime, the war had come to an end. As a result, the government canceled every order for equipment that it could, but was forced to take delivery of some electrical generators built for installation in destroyers. This led the government to sell these generators at almost give-away prices. TAPCO found a way to benefit from these low-priced generators. There were two significant lumber mills in northern Arizona that "hogged" their waste, meaning they burned their own mill waste. TAPCO could burn the ongoing waste of other businesses for fuel at very low acquisition cost, in comparison with other power sources, such as coal. TAPCO built so-called Dutch oven furnaces that burned the lumber mill waste to produce steam, which powered these war-excess generators to meet the electrical needs of the mills. When TAPCO generated the power to meet the need of the mills, any excess power generation was fed into its transmission line to the town of Show Low, Arizona and up to Holbrook.

Show Low was also an interesting opportunity for TAPCO. It was a small Mormon community where the Works Progress Administration had built a dam on a little creek going through the town to provide irrigation and power. Given shifts in the geologic substructure somewhere, the residents of Show Low awoke one morning to find that there was no water behind the dam. As a result, Show Low had a power emergency and brought in some noisy, old diesel-powered generators to provide emergency power to the community. In desperation, Show Low's city council called TAPCO, and I went down and met with the Mormons and made a deal to service the power needs of the community. Power would be generated at the Southwest Lumber Company plant in McNary or from the main transmission line running to Holbrook. Show Low issued bonds to finance the building of a transmission line from TAPCO's transmission line across northern Arizona to Show Low so that TAPCO only needed to build an extension on that line down to Southwest's lumber plant in McNary. The bonds were sold to Bank of America. This transaction was my first contact with the Bank of America. It also was my first experience in promoting the issuance and sale of tax-exempt bonds.

About a year before the Show Low deal, Jim Tucker withdrew from the Barcus, Kindred partnership. As a result, my carried interest in both TAPCO and in subsequent transactions I initiated was increased by the partnership. Also, at about this time, Ed Prince, a bond salesman for Barcus, Kindred, was meeting in the Celtic Bar of the Hotel Sherman in Chicago with Ray Braunburger, a salesman for Crucible Steel Casting in Milwaukee. Braunburger mentioned to Prince that he thought his employer, the Lange family that owned Crucible, would

probably be interested in selling their foundry. Prince reported this to Barcus.

It was 1944, a year after we had purchased the Arizona utili-
ties. Kindred thought: "Well, Colburn has worked for Columbia
Steel; he ought to know a little bit about the foundry business."
So he told me about the situation and suggested I look into it.
I then met Braunburger through Prince, the bond salesman,
and took a Northwestern Railway train with Braunburger from
Chicago up to Milwaukee. Walter Lange, president of Crucible,
met us at the train station and took us to a restaurant for lunch.

In the course of that lunch, Lange confirmed that he, his
two brothers, and one sister would be interested in selling
Crucible. One of the unique features of the company's situation, he said, was that he had an arrangement with twenty-one
employees, including a superintendent and other key people,
to return to him $18,000 a month in cash from their salaries,
which he was paying them in cash. He said the company was
paying excess profit tax at ninety-two percent, so he was getting that money at the employee's average tax rate of about
thirty-five percent. He said he prepared their income tax returns, paid their taxes, and filed the necessary reports with
the government on the payments and taxes withheld.

I could smell real trouble ahead for Lange. It was incred-
ibly stupid of him to have this arrangement, and also to tell
me about it. The day eventually came in 1947 when I sat on
the witness stand and reported what I knew to F. Ryan Duffy,
a former U.S. Senator then serving as a federal judge for the
eastern district of Wisconsin. However, at that lunch in 1944, I
told Lange that I was sure my associates would not like such an
arrangement. I went back and reported this fraud to my principals. Since we could change Lange's arrangement, I suggested

I be given authority to negotiate a purchase of the foundry business, which I received and executed.

In June 1944, the partners of Barcus, Kindred purchased Crucible, depositing the stock of Crucible along with $25,000 in escrow to secure the payment of the purchase price. Again, I had a carried interest. The contract provided that the price would be set by Price Waterhouse with an audit of Crucible spelling out in detail the basis for setting the purchase price with only one indeterminate element—the accrued, but not yet determined, amount of federal income taxes. With that contract, we took control of Crucible, and on June 19, 1944, I walked into Crucible's office as its new president, a few days before my thirty-third birthday. Among the first people I met were Mr. Cakkage, an Internal Revenue Agent, and Mr. Ream, an intelligence officer, who were sent in because fraud was suspected. I also met "Cowboy" Reed, a representative of the War Production Board, who was there to enforce compliance by Crucible in the scheduling of war production programs. Crucible had been giving priority to the production of castings for United Crane and Shovel Company. A significant portion of the payment for these castings was not recorded in Crucible's accounting records.

When I became Crucible's president, the company had just entered into a contract with the United Steel Workers, which had won a representation election. Most people wouldn't work in a foundry unless they had a strong back and a weak mind; the work was strenuous and unpleasant. A foundry is one of the worst environments in which one can work. It is not quite as unpleasant as a tannery or a slaughterhouse, but there is a lot of sand in the air and it is hot.

I noticed fairly quickly that castings were piled up to the crane rails in the cleaning room. The quickest way to liquidate an inventory backlog is to expedite the processes required to move the product through its remaining operations. Employees were all working at a straight hourly rate without any incentive to expedite or increase the level of their productivity. So, an industrial engineer was hired to do time studies of the various operations and to determine how to pay the employees for the amount of work produced, not for the number of hours they were on the job. If an employee could not do enough work on a shift to have earned at least his hourly rate, he had "to speed up or be shipped out." With the introduction of piece rates, Crucible was able to reduce its man-hours per-ton by almost twenty-five percent, which permitted increased production and lower cost, leading to increased profits. In the metals business you can shape a material by casting, forging, rolling, welding, or extruding it. These are the basic processes. Crucible made castings by pouring molten steel into a sand mold to make a particular shape. This method is used to make odd shapes. An example of a steel casting is a sprocket that turns the treads of a crawler tractor, or the treads themselves, which also are frequently cast.

From 1944 until 1947, for three years after we bought Crucible, I literally worked seven days a week—five of them as president at Crucible and two of them at TAPCO. During the sixty-five-mile, one-hour drive from my home and family in Winnetka to Crucible in southern Milwaukee, I would plan my day, thinking of the things I would do or say. As I drove home at night, I thought of the things I had said or done and of the things I should have said or done—and what I would do the following morning. Flying back and forth to TAPCO in

Arizona, my sleep was interspersed with similar thoughts about what had been done and what should be done.

In 1947, the Internal Revenue Service (IRS) filed a tax assessment and concurrently put a lien against the company's assets for back taxes. The size of the assessment was far more than the company was worth because the Langes had done so many improper things. The brothers and the brother-in-law, who was the chief financial officer, were indicted for filing false and fraudulent corporate and personal income tax returns. Of course we knew this was coming, so on the day when the IRS levied its assessment and filed the lien, Crucible filed a petition for reorganization under Chapter 11 of the Federal Bankruptcy Act. We concurrently asked that the court leave the company in possession, which was granted, subject to the appointment of a trustee to oversee the continuing operation of the company by its management.

As promptly as possible after filing for reorganization, Crucible presented its plan to the court. At the initial hearing on our proposal, our plan was bitterly opposed by a group of scrap dealers. Derald Ruttenberg, a thirty-year-old Yale Law School graduate, with an undergraduate degree from the University of Wisconsin, represented the dealers. He was with Moses, Bachrach & Kennedy, a prominent Chicago law firm.

Ruttenberg made a very persuasive argument to Judge Duffy that Barcus, Kindred should be disqualified from running Crucible because, he claimed, Barcus, Kindred did not come in with clean hands and Barcus, Kindred was just fronting for the Langes. The fact that Barcus, Kindred put up in escrow only $25,000 and the stock of Crucible was, he said, virtually proof that there really was no sale. Ruttenberg argued that nobody in his right mind would turn over a big business like Crucible to a bunch of pawn dealers for only $25,000. Judge Duffy listened attentively and asked questions. I thought that the judge was being pretty well convinced by this young lawyer. At that first hearing I assumed, "Boy, we're cooked cookies. We're going to get knocked out." But then I thought that maybe we could find some way for the scrap dealers to get knocked out. I told my principals about the situation and they gave me approval to seek some kind of settlement with Ruttenberg's clients.

I introduced myself to "Rutt," the nickname I gave to Ruttenberg. I worked to get to know him and to explain the merits of our plan. My effort, in turn, convinced Rutt to persuade the scrap dealers to support Crucible's reorganization plan. It had not yet come out in the trial that the scrap dealers also were up to their ears in part of the fraud—a couple of them deeply. It came out later in the trial that steel scrap was price-controlled at $35 a ton, and that the dealers got only a dollar commission for every ton sold. However, Walter Lange also paid the dealers a dollar a ton for some scrap that was never delivered. We never knew how much of the $35 a ton was kept by the dealers and how much was kicked back to the Langes. I remember the day when one of the scrap dealers, Zeek Arnowitz, was on the stand. The judge said to Arnowitz, "You may not be proud of what you're going to have to tell the court. But you've taken an oath to tell the truth, the whole truth, and nothing but the truth. And you've got to be very sure that you do that." Arnowitz told the judge that he got a lot of money for tons he never delivered and that he'd given a fair amount of that money back to the Lange family, mostly to Walter Lange. That one bit of testimony convicted the Langes.

Of course, I also was on the witness stand. I remember feeling uncomfortable with the Langes sitting there looking at me while I was testifying before Judge Duffy about the kickback arrangement Walter had told me about back in 1944. Walter had periodically made trips to Cuba or Jamaica, and it is likely that he had his suitcase filled with currency. Anyway, the Lange brothers and the brother-in-law were convicted and sentenced to extended terms in prison, except for Abe Lange, who collapsed on the stand. They found he had inoperable throat cancer. He died soon thereafter. He never went to the penitentiary, but other members of the family did.

After this trial, our reorganization plan was accepted, and we paid our creditors what we said we would. By far the biggest creditor was the IRS. I made a trip with Richard Meyer to Washington to meet with the general counsel for the IRS. We went into the office of the assistant attorney general, who was in charge of the IRS legal section. He greeted us, was very cordial, and the first thing he did was to thank us for our cooperation "with my government." I asked, "Your government?" He said, "That's right. It never wants to kill the goose that lays the golden egg."

The government settled reasonably with Crucible, and within sixty days Crucible had paid back the government with the help of a bank loan. In 120 days, my principals had their $25,000 back, along with all the other money they had advanced the company. Barcus, Kindred got the company for very little, and I owned eight percent of Crucible. Moreover, once Crucible was able to borrow an amount sufficient to pay off the government and other creditors in accordance with the reorganization plan, Crucible was free and clear of pre-Chapter 11 debts.

After our purchase of Crucible was settled in late 1947 or early 1948, we started buying other foundries. I invited Rutt to start working with me. As a result, Rutt and I worked together on many deals over the years. Our first acquisition—one identified by Rutt—was Eboloy, a sand-cast and permanent-mold aluminum foundry in Rockford, Illinois. Our next acquisition was that of Michigan Steel Casting Company, headquartered in Detroit, Michigan, whose two principal shareholders were John Charles Redmond and Cloud Cray. Redmond controlled the Mack Truck account, Michigan Steel's largest customer, and Cray was an alcohol distiller from Topeka, Kansas.

Michigan Steel Casting Company was engaged in four different businesses. One was the sand-mold casting of high-nickel chrome alloys that provided resistance to exceptionally high temperatures, and was therefore used in the construction of heat-treating furnaces. A second business was the production in silica molds of nickel-chrome-cobalt alloy products having high strength, exceptionally high heat resistance, and very smooth surfaces. These castings were used in various aircraft engine parts, such as buckets for the superchargers of radial engines built by Curtis-Wright, and blades and vanes for jet engines, initially for Pratt & Whitney and later for General Electric and Rolls-Royce. The process is akin to the lost-wax process for casting bronze statues and tooth inlays. We produced the first such castings for the initial commercial jet engines, and this grew to become an enormous business. The third business was the distribution of rolled-nickel chrome alloy steel plate, beams, rods, and tubes that are used in high-temperature applications and frequently used in fabrication involving both rolled and cast nickel-chrome steel. The fourth business was the fabrication of products employing both high nickel-chrome cast and rolled steel material welded together.

Shortly after the purchase of Michigan Steel, we divided the company into four separate units to conduct the aforementioned four different activities. These were named: Michigan Steel Casting Company, Misco Precision Casting Company, Rolled Alloys, Inc., and Misco Fabricators, Inc. This restructuring was in part motivated by the tax laws, which provided a low federal tax on a company's first $25,000 of income. Concurrently, we set up different companies that owned the real estate and facilities employed by each of these companies. At this same time, we brought into being Consolidated Foundries as the owner of Crucible Steel in Milwaukee; Eboloy in Rockford; Michigan Steel Casting in both Detroit and Whitehall, Michigan; Misco Precision Casting Company in Whitehall; and Rolled Alloys and Misco Fabricators, both in Detroit. After we owned these businesses a year or two, we discontinued the operation of Misco Fabricators because that company was in direct competition with fabricator customers of Michigan Steel Casting Company and Rolled Alloys, a situation we found to be counterproductive.

Our next acquisition was that of Western Foundry, a gray iron foundry having plants in the town of Holland, Michigan and in Chicago. We immediately closed the Chicago plant and sold off the real estate, which had more value as real estate than as a foundry. Our next acquisition was that of Crucible Steel Casting Company in Cleveland, Ohio, bearing the same name as the foundry in Milwaukee, but with no ties other than an identical name. Its principal customer was Powell Valves in Cincinnati. Consolidated Foundries then acquired Adirondack Steel Casting in Watervliet, New York, whose principal customers were the builders of railroad freight and passenger car frames and locomotive frames for General Electric.

In the acquisition of these foundries, I negotiated the purchase terms and Rutt worked out the details of the contracts with the sellers' counsel. Together we were a great team. We successfully introduced the same piecework incentive program at Western Foundry that we had installed at Crucible in Milwaukee, at Crucible in Cleveland, and at Adirondack in Watervliet. Each foundry operated as a stand-alone business with its own president and staff. The presidents and chief financial officers each reported directly to me. I felt that the accountant should never just speak to the president of the unit, but should report independently to the board of directors, which, in practice, was almost solely me, except on critically important issues for which I sought the concurrence of Rutt and Kindred. I learned about the foundry business by looking and listening. I could clearly see what every workman did, and I asked questions endlessly. My father told me as a boy that an inquiring mind is the first mark of intelligence. The more questions one asks, the more one will learn.

In about 1948, I asked Henry Sargent, the president of CALAPCO, the electrical utility in Phoenix, if CALAPCO might be interested in the purchase of TAPCO. His response was an emphatic "yes," so I then sought the concurrence of Barcus, Kindred and, of course, Rutt. Shortly thereafter, a group of us met every day for almost a week in the penthouse of the Westward Ho Hotel in Phoenix. We moved the dining room table into the living room, set up three secretarial desks and equipment in the dining room, and started drafting a contract for the sale of TAPCO assets to CALAPCO. Our group was assisted by an attorney from Chicago, Lou Hardin. The only assets excluded were the hydroelectric plants on federal land, which would have subjected CALAPCO to the jurisdiction of the Federal Power Commission.

On the completion of the TAPCO asset sale to CALAPCO, Hardin made a visit to the Grand Canyon and sent postcards to Rutt and me saying, "Son-of-a-bitch! What a ditch!" One year later, Prince, the bond salesman for Barcus, Kindred who was instrumental in bringing the Crucible-Milwaukee acquisition to our attention, sold the remaining hydroelectric plants to the Czechoslovak Society of America, a fraternal insurance company. I made a handsome profit from the sale of TAPCO.

In 1955, I asked my wife Elizabeth for a divorce. We didn't have separate lawyers. Lou Hardin worked out our settlement agreement. I became close to Joan Garber, who had been my secretary at Crucible Steel Casting Company. One day, when Joan and I were driving from California to Milwaukee, we stopped in Winnemucca, Nevada, and got a marriage license—we were married in a matter of ten or fifteen minutes. Then we got back in the car and continued driving. Our first child was Christine Isabel Colburn; she was followed by David Colburn; and then there was a second son, whom we named Texas McKee Colburn. To this day he's called "Tex," although his birth was recorded in the name McKee Dunton Colburn. We called him Texas McKee because the day he was born I was in Texas purchasing an electrical distribution business from the Robert McKee family in El Paso, Texas. All three children were born in California. Joan and I divorced in 1964.

Sometime prior to 1961, when Barcus was in his seventies, he retired from the bond business and concurrently sold his interest in Consolidated Foundries back to the company. Later, in 1961, Rutt also wanted to sell his interest in Consolidated

Foundries so he could pursue other projects. Meanwhile, Rutt had found a buyer for one of our units, Misco Precision Casting Company. The consummation of this sale gave Consolidated Foundries the cash with which to repurchase Rutt's interest.

Given the benefit of hindsight, I know I was seriously mistaken in supporting the sale of Misco Precision Casting Company to Howe Sound, a mining company of which Bill Weaver was president. The investment casting products Howe Sound obtained from Misco then became the overwhelming part of its business and grew to over a billion dollars a year in sales. I didn't see the dramatic growth of the jet engine business that was soon to occur and would continue. Shortly thereafter, General Electric and Rolls-Royce joined Pratt & Whitney in the production of jet engines and became Misco customers.

Prior to Rutt's withdrawing in 1961, he, Barcus, Kindred, and I purchased U.S. Brewing from its thirty-five employee shareholders. They had inherited the company from a deceased former owner, who had also owned Pabst and thirteen other breweries. U.S. Brewing had become the victim of several years of constant management turnover because of shifting allegiances of the shareholders. Among U.S. Brewing's assets were the sole rights to use the Löwenbräu beer name in the United States, except in those states facing the Atlantic, the Pacific, and the Caribbean. At Kindred's insistence, we discontinued the brewing of beer within thirty days and promptly sold for a good price the bottling and brew house equipment, as well as the rights to the Löwenbräu name. Within a year, we also sold the real estate, except for the property on which stood Available Truck, a trucking subsidiary that manufactured custom truck chassis and power trains. Within a few years we sold Available Truck to Bucyrus-Erie. This company mounted the cranes, backhoes, and related earth-moving products it manufactured on Available Truck chassis and power trains.

On June 30, 1964, by means of a tax-free spin-off, Rolled Alloys and an "equalizing" amount of cash were transferred to me from Consolidated Foundries to retire my interest in the company. Kindred then was left as the sole owner of the Consolidated Foundries. In the interim, between Rutt's withdrawal and my buyout, Kindred replaced Rutt with a Mr. Phillips, an experienced "foundry man." While I retained my title and compensation, I was effectively reduced to a minor role in the management of Consolidated Foundries. This transition was sixteen years after the sale of TAPCO, so I said—for a number of years—that "I got out of jail" after serving Barcus, Kindred for over twenty years. I was a free man! I was the sole shareholder of Rolled Alloys and was earning over $500,000 a year after corporate taxes in addition to my salary. I was also well prepared to now work, in "stand-alone" fashion, as an entrepreneur.

In working as an entrepreneur, I was to be fortified by what I had learned from working with TAPCO and Consolidated Foundries. I learned several important lessons. Lesson one: What one personally thinks is never as important as what the other party thinks, because the other person's actions will usually be in harmony with what they think. The challenge is to discern what they think, why they think it, what should I say to bring their thoughts in harmony with mine, or how should I change my thoughts to bring myself into harmony with their thoughts. If people fail to reach agreement, it is often because neither party can discern what the other party is thinking and then cannot, through compromise, achieve an agreement.

Lesson two: When in negotiations, if you state clearly what you are willing to do and then compromise so as to change what you are willing to do, you have made a liar out of yourself.

Lesson three: When purchasing a business nothing is more important than to buy right. You shouldn't pay more for a business than the price from which one can reasonably expect to earn at least one dollar more than what one paid under the worse circumstances.

Lesson four: Buy; never sell. The only significant mistakes I ever made were in selling. I cannot think of any business or property we sold that we would not have been better off having held for the long term, presuming continuity of competent management. I remember Jim Barcus saying to me over and over again, "Dick, you'll never go broke taking a profit," and that concept is correct. However, one has to pay tax on the profits, and one has to find something else good in which to reinvest the after-tax profits. Markets go up, markets go down, so at one time I thought "buy cheap, sell dear," but much later I gave that maxim up and determined I was better off with the philosophy of "buy, never sell."

Lesson five: Never permit an employee to fire an immediate subordinate without the concurrence of higher authority.

Lesson six: Success is the compounded result of doing a great many little things well. The "big things," because they are big and important, tend to be well taken care of. However, while details tend not to be too important individually, in the aggregate they are the compounding determinant of the success or failure of every undertaking. I learned that the critical issues in a contract could be in the fine print. Just three lines—or less—can make an enormous difference.

There is a difference between a manager and an entrepreneur. Being a successful manager does not in and of itself make one a capable entrepreneur. However, you cannot be a successful entrepreneur if you are not a skilled manager.

CHAPTER 6

# Being an Entrepreneur

AFTER I TERMINATED MY RELATIONSHIP with Barcus, Kindred in June of 1964, Rutt and I again became investment partners with identical fifty-fifty interests in whatever we did. Rutt had been making a number of personal investments, including the Illinois Iron and Bolt Company of Carpentersville, Illinois that originally was founded by my maternal grandfather, Delos Dunton. As far as I know, it was just by coincidence that Ruttenberg purchased the company.

By 1964, Rutt also had invested in Worthington Pump, an independent company whose chairman was Walter Feldman. From Feldman, Rutt learned about and became interested in Tung-Sol. The company produced glass and metal-sealed products, such as radio vacuum tubes, headlights, light bulbs, and smaller light bulbs for automobile dashboards and courtesy lamps. Rutt and I invested in the company. We subsequently invested in Wagner Electric, Studebaker-Worthington, and Susquehanna.

In addition to sealed beam headlamps and tubes for radio sets, Tung-Sol had the patent for the so-called flasher, which was a turn-signal indicator. At that time I remember Frank Ehringer, the president of Tung-Sol, telling me that transistors would be a flash in the pan. He believed there was no way that the transistor would replace the vacuum tube. As a result we had some trouble persuading him that he was losing money making vacuum tubes, and that Tung-Sol should get out of that business because the transistor was rapidly replacing the vacuum tube. After eventually discontinuing the unprofitable manufacturing of vacuum tubes, and then expanding the sales of so called "courtesy lamps" for automobiles, such as headlights, taillight tubes, and dashboard lights, the company returned to profitability.

During our 1964 investment in Tung-Sol, the participation of a friend of Rutt's, Nathan Cummings, permitted us to gain a controlling interest in the company. Walter Feldman also helped us by purchasing some of the Tung-Sol shares. Cummings was a friend of Rutt's uncle who had a bakery on the North Side of Chicago that produced Sara Lee coffee cakes. At about the same time as the Tung-Sol deal, Rutt's uncle got a "big piece" of Sara Lee, and it was through Rutt's uncle that Rutt and I bought into Sara Lee.

Rutt had another friend, Peter Forman, who worked for a brokerage firm. Forman told Rutt that Wagner Electric was a great company, but that it was losing its shirt making transformers and that we ought to buy it and improve its operations. Since Wagner Electric was a publicly traded company, Tung-Sol was able to start buying Wagner Electric stock with the money that we freed up by getting out of the business of making vacuum tubes for radios and TV sets. We then prevailed upon Tung-Sol to make a tender offer for Wagner Electric stock. We didn't acquire all the stock, but we got enough to merge the two companies and change the name of Tung-Sol to Wagner Electric. So Tung-Sol's business continued under the Wagner name. In addition to transformers, Wagner produced brakes and brake fluid.

About this time, Rutt moved to New York City, and we shared an office in the building just south of the Waldorf Astoria.

Felix Rohatyn was also in this building with Lazard Frères. It was Felix Rohatyn who came and talked to us about merging Wagner into Studebaker as a means of avoiding a proxy battle. Soon thereafter, we merged Wagner into Studebaker, and that move considerably diluted Rutt's and my financial interest in the resulting company. Upon the merger, Rutt became the president of Studebaker-Worthington, a position he held until the 1979 sale of the company to McGraw-Edison. At that time, Studebaker-Worthington was already out of the automobile business. They owned STP, the oil additive. They also made portable generator units for institutions, schools, hospitals, and office buildings.

In 1972, Rutt and I, along with Henry Crown, acquired Susquehanna, a mini-conglomerate. Rutt knew Crown through our involvement with him in purchasing shares in Sara Lee. I became the non-executive chairman of Susquehanna and, to run the mini-conglomerate as its president, I recruited Jerry Kean. We bought the control of Susquehanna from Herb Korholz, its chief executive, who has been immortalized in the book *In the Name of Profit: Profiles in Corporate Irresponsibility.* His business practices and ethics were incompatible with my own.

I never had a written agreement with Rutt. We had a strong relationship and we talked every day—or every night. With him in New York and me in Los Angeles, he might call me at 7:00 am, which was 4:00 am for me. I, however, sometimes called him at 11:00 pm, 2:00 am for him. Rutt was the "big-picture man," and I was the "detail man." We formed a complementary team. Rutt sold Studebaker-Worthington to McGraw-Edison in 1979 for cash. As it worked out, it was a timely deal because we got our money out just before a market downturn.

During the period when I was working with Barcus, Kindred and with Rutt, I was also acquiring businesses on my own. After

Rutt and I parted, I continued to make such acquisitions. I became an entrepreneur, drawing on skills I had learned from working as a manager. I also returned to my native California and made it my home.

Since leaving San Diego in 1929 to attend Antioch College, I had a somewhat subconscious desire to return "to the womb," to come back to California. When one of my Chicago colleagues moved from Chicago to San Francisco, I asked him to call me if he saw any business opportunities there that might be of interest to me. I had had enough of Chicago's subzero winters and its hot, high-humidity summers. I eventually received a call from him in 1957, advising me that the Bank of America had foreclosed on San Francisco Electric Supply Company due to a loan default. This company operated warehouses in San Francisco and Oakland. They were engaged in the distribution of electrical construction and maintenance materials and industrial, commercial, and residential lighting products.

On a weekend trip in 1957 to San Francisco to evaluate San Francisco Electric Supply, I also learned about the possibility of acquiring Phillips & Edwards Electric Supply Company, a distributor of electrical construction maintenance materials with warehouses in San Francisco, Redwood City, and Stockton. I purchased San Francisco Electric Supply Company on September 17, by which time I had also reached an agreement to purchase Phillips & Edwards on September 30. This second deal was financed by a loan from the Bank of America, secured by my stock in Consolidated Foundries. Upon the purchases of these two businesses, I consolidated the stocking of electrical construction materials for both companies at the Phillips & Edwards warehouse in San Francisco and left the lighting products business as it was. I then combined the offices of these two businesses in a building on Mission Street in San Francisco.

The price a manufacturer charged a distributor was determined by the quantity ordered, so to get the lowest price, one frequently had to purchase as much as a six-month's supply of an item. After the combination of San Francisco Electric Supply and Phillips & Edwards, we almost doubled our volume, and the inventory turnover of the consolidated business was also significantly improved. With one less company in the business in the San Francisco area, there was also a slight improvement in pricing, higher gross profit, and lower costs. After our consolidation we had only one president, one sales manager, and a single salesman, instead of two, calling on each customer. We also had only one switchboard operator instead of two, one inventory to control instead of two, one purchasing agent instead of two, and somewhat fewer accounts receivable ledgers because both companies were frequently selling to the same customer. The consolidated company was called Phillips & Edwards, and its switchboard operator answered calls saying, "Phillips & Edwards, not the biggest, but the best."

The consolidation of San Francisco Electric Supply and Phillips & Edwards was the beginning of an extended period during which I built a substantial company that distributes electrical equipment. I changed the name, the organizational structure, and just about everything else, but, most significantly I added dozens of different branches, many by the acquisition of other more local or regional companies. And I moved the base of the company from northern California to Los Angeles, where I moved myself on May 1, 1965. However, I was still involved in business dealings in New York. One year, in fact, I made forty-six trips to New York. And I traveled elsewhere, since I had a commitment to visit every plant and office of all of the businesses I owned. I worked hard.

Working at efficiently—and profitably—distributing electrical equipment led to other acquisitions, one of which was a major distributor of electrical equipment in Great Britain. This move introduced the challenge of operating in a different cultural, as well as geographical, setting. A loan officer at the Bank of America told me that while profit sharing worked well for me here in the United States, the British were not motivated as much by money. He said, "Their afternoon tea is more important than an extra pound." I proved him wrong. Another notable acquisition was in the United States, Leasing Enterprises, centered on the West Coast. It rented construction equipment, from small cement mixers to bulldozers.

In Los Angeles, I settled on La Collina, a quiet street in Beverly Hills. My residence came to be known to family members and friends just as "La Collina." I lived in a number of adjacent houses on the street, before designing my own home. I did the basic floor plan. I didn't have a model, but I did know that the most important room in the house was the music room— and I made it large. Everything else about the house was secondary. The property came with a modest pool house, which I made into a guesthouse. I also built an office. I bought the fireplace hearths, mantels, and facings for the master bedroom, music room, and library from the William Randolph Hearst Estate. Almost everything else I bought in Europe. One of my favorite pieces of furniture is a narrow refractory table, which I used as a dining table. It is from a monastery in Florence. The monks sat on one side and were served from the other side of the table. There is a board at the base, and the monks would put their feet on the board to avoid the cold stone floors of the monastery.

I never wanted to own an airplane—and I never did. I never played tennis or golf, or joined a country club. But I have always lived comfortably, and I have always enjoyed beautiful music. I entertain often at my home, and I have long opened my doors to musicians and conductors who come to Los Angeles to perform. Some of my most memorable occasions have been dinner parties held to give financial supporters of the Los Angeles Philharmonic an opportunity to meet the soloists and to encourage supporters to continue their gifts. I have three tables to press into service, and can seat as many as thirty-eight—and we often have a full house. Great musicians have been guests, including: Alfred Brendel, Esa-Pekka Salonen, Yehudi Menuhin, Mstislav Rostropovich, Isaac Stern, Valery Gergiev, Mikhail Pletnev, Christian Thielemann, Siegfried Jerusalem, Plácido Domingo, Kent Nagano, Gregor Piatigorsky, Jascha Heifetz, Lynn Harrell, Zubin Mehta, Jimmy Galway, Neville Marriner, Barry Tuckwell, and Yo-Yo Ma. We have had a great time, and often great music, too.

I remember with glee one night when many of the guests ended up in the pool, some still in their concert attire and others with little or no attire. Malcolm Hamilton, the harpsichordist, was standing out by the pool. I said, "What's the matter, Malcolm? Why aren't you in there? He held his tuxedo lapels between his fingers and said, "I have to play a concert in two nights; I can't go in there." I said, "I'll buy you a new tux." So he jumped in—and he didn't even take his shoes off or bother to take anything out of his pockets. His manager, who was sitting inside the pavilion (as we called the guesthouse), came running outside, yelling, "Malcolm! Malcolm! What are you doing?" Everyone laughed and laughed. I bought Malcolm a new tux.

As busy—and as healthy—as I was, I kept in the back of my mind a conversation I had in 1957 with my lawyer, Lou Hardin. He said to me that I should do two things. First, I should "plan to live forever," but second, I should also be prepared to die in an instant. I said, "No problem. I have that all worked out. I plan to live forever." He said, "And so do I, Dick, but there's a remote possibility something might happen." This meeting took place on the seventieth floor of the Sears Tower in Chicago, and the building was swaying a little bit in the wind. (Chicago gets some pretty good winds.) It was a corner office with plate glass. Hardin said, "An airplane could come crashing into the room here, and you and I would never get out of this room alive." I said, "Yes, I agree." He said, "What are you going to do about it? Do you know what it is going to cost you to die?"

Hardin persuaded me that I should start giving away what I had until I reduced my net worth to what the British call "a sufficiency." In 1972, I turned over the day-to-day management of many of the businesses I then owned to my older children and, with Hardin's counsel, I transferred to my children an interest in the businesses, too. However, I continued to manage—and own—the last major acquisition I had made, Leasing Enterprises. I purchased that company in about 1979, which would have meant I was sixty-eight years old at the time. Three years later I changed the name to U.S. Rentals. I managed the company, and worked diligently to "grow it," to increase its presence by opening new branch offices. I ran the firm for nineteen years, until I was eighty-eight. At that point, in 1997, at the urging of Bill Berry and John McKinney, then president and chief financial officer of U.S. Rentals, I sold thirty percent of the stock of the company in an initial public offering. Berry and McKinney were concerned about what would happen to them and to U.S. Rentals if it was still a private company at the time of my demise, which I believe they expected would be sooner than I had planned. A year later, in 1998, I agreed to the merger of U.S. Rentals into United Rentals, a public company listed on the New York Stock Exchange. I, in effect, sold U.S. Rentals. I had not planned on selling the company, but I was offered a staggering sum of money. I had long observed that "markets go up, markets go down." I could only conclude that "markets were up." I took the money and let go of the company.

With the sale of U.S. Rentals, I became, at age eighty-nine, unemployed. I had always coveted a high degree of privacy about my business affairs, which was lost taking U.S. Rentals public and then merging it with United Rentals. These transactions did, however, help me bring into being two foundations to which I have gifted most of my net worth. I have retained an amount sufficient to enable me to live out the remaining years of my life in reasonable comfort.

Since leaving business, I have concentrated on my charitable activities. In 1999, I established the Colburn Foundation, and in 2001, I established the Colburn Music Fund. I had long believed not only in supporting the performance of beautiful music, but in the need for a top-flight school of music education on the West Coast of the United States. My success in business enabled me to provide needed support for established musical organizations and, moreover, to provide the "seed money" for a new musical school in Los Angeles. The Colburn Music Fund was established solely to provide needed financing for what would come to be the Colburn School. The purpose of the Colburn Foundation is both to provide assistance to the school and to support the performance of music in Los Angeles, and elsewhere.

I am pleased that my children, who are now adults, are managing the assets I transferred to them with a high degree of prudence. They worked with me in some of the businesses I owned, and so did my brother Price, who earlier had worked for my other brother, William. Now my children carry on, not just with what I have left them, but with what I taught them. I'm not in close touch anymore with their financial affairs; I've not meddled. I've given them the right to be wrong. The worst thing I know is for a father to hang on too long. They have done well without me. They share my values of hard work, of husbanding resources carefully, and, also, of making, in due time, a contribution—however they wish—to society. I am well aware, though, that rarely do business families go successfully into the third generation: as the saying goes, "shirtsleeves to shirtsleeves in three generations."

One of my sons, and I would like to believe he was speaking for all of my children (and so I won't give his name), offered a succinct—and gratifying—summary of my approach to business:

*My father, who we often refer to as "RDC," had six tenets in business.*

*Number one: He always focused on buying what I would term mundane businesses. They weren't complicated business enterprises. The businesses were fairly easy to understand. They typically had a lot of assets, and, therefore, were able to be leveraged through bank debt. But the key is that they were relatively simple businesses to understand. He owned multi-location manufacturing and wholesaling businesses that provided basic industrial products and services to local customers.*

*The second tenet was decentralization. My father felt that one should empower managers by pushing authority and responsibility down to the line level, that is, the profit-center level. One of the things that he would say in this regard is that he "turns managers into businessmen." It's a good encapsulation of what decentralization is all about: the idea of allowing the managers to control their own destinies and entering into a relationship where my father really is like a banker. In other words, he has the role of financier. He lends them the assets that they need to run their business. He then charges an interest rate on those assets and agrees to split the profits. The key to the decentralization focus is that you have to let go. Some local managers may fail once or twice, and that might cost you some money, but you can't be halfway in decentralization. There are a lot of companies that say they're decentralized, but really aren't. They still have a lot of central corporate control. They still have a mentality that the supervisors know best and that they need to tell the local manager what to buy and to whom to sell. My father has a great belief in true decentralization.*

*The third tenet is that he had a strict focus on "return on investment." My father once said, "All wealth is created by arbitraging rates of return." That's such a simple notion, that all wealth is created by investing at a higher rate of return than your cost of funds. My father told me years ago that an early goal of his was to earn a twenty percent after-tax return. My father measures return on investment almost to the exclusion of all other metrics or ratios. He said that if you earn a twenty percent after-tax return, money doubles about every five years. In a forty-year business life you double your money eight times.*

*So you start with $100,000, and over eight, five-year periods you have, successively: $200,000, $400,000, $800,000, $1.6 million, $3.2 million, $6.4 million, $12.8 million, and $25.6 million. So, in forty years, you can turn $100,000 into almost $26 million if you earn a twenty percent after-tax return. And my father said to me he thought he could achieve that result. But, in fact, he did even better. I have found that few people really understand the idea of compounding rates of return. Many managers—and even entrepreneurs—are often so busy tied up in their world of managing the specifics of their particular business that they lose focus on the importance of rate of return and the importance of compounding returns. However, these concepts have been understood by my father.*

*The fourth tenet is systems and procedures. My father felt that in a decentralized business model, the principal risk you run is giving too much authority and responsibility to the wrong person. If you have a rogue manager, for example, you could lose a lot of money very quickly. So my father, at the same time that he had a decentralized focus, also had very strong measuring systems, procedures, and controls. The companies in which he had investments all had policy manuals, and they had put in place in-house audits and internal audit teams. These audit teams would effectively study the local branch and come up with an audit score. If the branch had a high return on investment but a low audit score, my father would feel ambivalent about the manager. He wouldn't necessarily praise him at the annual budget meetings. In fact, I remember what he once said to a manager who had a high return on investment but a poor internal audit score: the manager was talking about how much money he was planning to make in the coming year, and my father said, "Well, how would I know? How would I know that you made as much money as you report since your accounting is so poor?" A retort my father would use was, "I lack faith in your numbers."*

*My father believed strongly in measuring people and also in making sure that they were held accountable for following the systems and procedures that were put in place. My understanding is that my Uncle Price was very involved in setting up these systems and procedures. Obviously, it was my father's philosophy that Price was implementing, but I think that Price put it together. On the administration side, my father would say, "Plan your work and work your plan." That was the idea behind having these annual budgets that he would have his managers prepare and present to him. He would also say, "I'm just a poor old bean counter." What he meant, I think, is that his strength was not in managing the business, but in designing and monitoring the systems and procedures. I remember him saying at one point, and he was exaggerating to make a point: "When I walk into one of my warehouses, I really don't know what the product is on the shelf. I don't know what its end use is, but I understand the language of business and I understand accounting. I can read financial reports because I was trained as an accountant."*

*My father's first job in accounting was as an auditor, so he understood the importance of keeping score. My father believed strongly that the internal auditors should report to the owner, directly to him. In virtually every publicly traded company that you will ever encounter, the internal audit department, if there is one and very often there isn't, will report to the president. In other words, it will report to the person it is auditing. It will report to the person it is possibly going to be critical of. My father believed that while a dotted-line relationship is important to the president, the head of the internal audit should really report to and be beholden to the owner, the chairman of the board, or the controlling partner. That's key to my father, because of his sense that people can be, and are, filters of communication. When my father says: "Is there anything you know and I don't but should?" it is a serious question. The concern here is that if the internal auditor is reporting to the president, what portion of that information is actually going to be filtered before it gets up to the owner? Thus, it is best to remove that filter, and have the report go directly to my father—the owner; my father can later send it to the president. The president then has an opportunity to offer a response. It was Uncle Price who said, "Administration is an exercise in doubt." What Uncle Price meant is that when you look at a manager, you have to be skeptical, because managers act in their own self-interest and may not tell you everything. I would describe this part of my father's philosophy as doing due diligence on your own organization, digging, finding out more, and more, and more.*

*The fifth tenet is profit sharing. To reiterate, my father would play the role of a financier, would effectively lend these local managers assets to use in carrying out the trade of their business. They would then pay him for use of these assets. We call it an investment charge but it's really a rate of interest on those assets. Then they would share in the profits after that "interest" cost, including with people to whom they wanted to provide an incentive. These would be people who worked with the managers, their colleagues, as we like to say in our business. Not employees, not workers, but colleagues. In budget meetings, for emphasis my father used to say to a manager who maybe reported very good results for the year: "I'm disappointed in you. I'm disappointed you didn't make more money, because the more you make, the more I make." This remark would have a tremendous impact. It's the idea of spreading this philosophy that we're partners. I'm not the owner and you don't work for me. I lend you assets and you do the best you can to earn a high return on those assets. And if you earn a high enough return that you can pay my interest rate, then above that you start sharing in the profit.*

*The sixth tenet my father had was that enterprises must grow. He used to say, "If you're not growing, you're shrinking." What he meant by that, I think, is that one thing you can be sure of is that every year your expenses are going to go up. Expenses inexorably increase. Salaries go up, insurance costs go up, rent goes up, utility costs go up, and the cost of the product that you're selling goes up. In the manufacturing business, your cost of goods sold increases. So if you're not focused on growth, either organic growth on a same-store basis, or growth through acquisition, your enterprise value could shrink each year. More of the value of the enterprise will go to the creditors, because you'll have to borrow to pay your increasingly higher expenses. When my father was managing the principal business of the family, he would spend most of his time on acquisitions. The idea was that if he had properly structured his organization so that the managers were given incentives to earn high returns, and the auditors were given incentives to make sure the managers are kept in check, then he was free, to a great extent, to focus on larger strategic issues, such as how "to grow" the organization.*

*My father was always focused on acquiring businesses and then improving their "paper processing," as he would call it, which I would call their general and administrative expense, and consolidating it such that you were spreading it over a larger number of operating units. Therefore, as a percentage of revenue, that expense got smaller and smaller. A key approach he took to add value to the organizations he purchased and turned around was to consolidate the back room—the paper processing, the administrative functions, insurance, payroll, accounts receivable, accounts payable, all of the items that a manager of a business unit really did not need to manage directly. That consolidation had the impact of lowering expenses as a percentage of revenue, because, for example, you were taking a chief financial officer out of every single business unit. That step alone can save large amounts of money. And you were replacing that chief financial officer with at best a bookkeeper. But, in addition to lowering your expenses, you were also freeing up the manager's time to go out and sell.*

*A lot of my father's aphorisms dovetail into each of these six points of business philosophy. For example, he often says, "You really have to buy right." What RDC means is you should not overpay for a business because, if you pay a sensible price, you have more options if things go wrong. Another thing he used to say was, "You should buy so that the worst that could happen is that you make a dollar." This quip embodies the concept of paying a price that is sufficiently low that if things go very wrong, you can liquidate the business and get your investment back. And certainly in his early years, he did pay those types of low prices for decent businesses, even good businesses. It's virtually impossible to pay those kinds of prices nowadays. There's just more competition for acquisitions. It was part of his acquisition philosophy that he would walk away from a good business rather than overpay. My father once said, "The art of making money is spending wisely."*

*My father always wanted to know everything about his organization. I remember sitting in his office once when he had received an anonymous letter stating that a secretary in his organization was dating a vice president and that both were married. I didn't know how he was going to react. I thought it was possible that he would just throw it away and say, well, it was probably written by a disgruntled former employee. But he didn't. He took it very seriously. That letter sat on his desk for a few days. My understanding is that he called the vice president and asked him, "Is this report true?" I think the fellow denied it and then resigned a short time thereafter. So such details are important to my father, and little things didn't go unnoticed. In terms of fact-finding in this case, RDC would have employees he would call on and ask questions to get information about the goings-on in a particular area, for example, in a corporate headquarters. He would do a lot of digging. My father is a person who, I think, always felt you could never know enough about a situation. He has a very analytical mind and information is important to him.*

*What's also interesting about RDC is that as he accumulates information, he doesn't simply make a decision. Instead, there's a period during which he processes—mulls over—the information. He likes to say he's like a fly: no one ever knows where he's going to land. That's the way he is. And it's frustrating to people. In his dealings with people in music or in philanthropy, and in dealing with family members—myself included—there would be situations where there was the expectation that he was going to do something, but he didn't. I learned early in life to be patient when it came to RDC, because he took his time to think carefully about every situation. Until my father actually took an action that could not be revoked—by signing a contract or making an investment or a philanthropic donation—you never knew how he was going to end up on an issue. His mind—his thinking—is the key to his success in business. However, it is not just raw intelligence, though that he has, but his disciplined, methodical manner of thinking. Richard D. Colburn is a master at the art of business.*

CHAPTER 7

# Music

MUSIC HAS ALWAYS BEEN AN important part of my life since I was
a boy. Now, so many decades later, I go almost every year to
the Easter Festival in the little town of Naarden, which is about
twenty miles outside of Amsterdam. Naarden is a charming
village surrounded by a moat. There is no structure over two
stories high, except the church steeple, which you can see from
ten to fifteen miles away because the land is as flat as a pan-
cake. For over 250 years on Good Friday, Bach's *St. Matthew
Passion* has been performed at the village church, originally built in the thirteenth century. It is my annual visit to a
church. During the church service, I sit in a pew and think of
the generations of men and women who have sat there before
me and heard the same great music performed on instruments
of the period. Neither the singers nor the instrumentalists use
vibrato. The music is beautiful. I love it. The first part of the
performance is from eleven o'clock in the morning until about
twelve-thirty in the afternoon. Afterwards, I go out and have
lunch in one of the little restaurants in the village. I return to
the church later for the remainder of the performance.

The love I have of music comes from having heard classical music at home as an integral part of my childhood. The first music

I remember hearing as a boy was Amelita Galli-Curci, a great operatic soprano. We had a Victrola in our house, and we had some Victor records, one of which was of Galli-Curci singing. The first recording of Jascha Heifetz I remember hearing was the *Chorus of the Dervishes*. I used to sit and listen to it over and over. We didn't have the recording at home, but my Uncle Cecil and Aunt Myrtle had it in their home. Radios weren't widely available until I was in my teens. The first radio music I remember hearing was Arturo Toscanini with the New York Philharmonic. So, I heard good music growing up, though I wouldn't say my parents personally brought much music into our home. My father couldn't sing "The Star-Spangled Banner," and he was virtually tone deaf. However, my mother played the piano, and when I started to take violin lessons, she had a violin of her own and would practice with me. And both of my brothers also had music lessons. Playing violin enhanced my interest in listening to music, and listening to beautiful music deepened my desire to make music myself.

When I listen to music, I frequently try to anticipate the next chord and maybe even the following one. In other words: where are they going? It is like a conversation, when someone asks you a question. How you respond to the question has to be influenced by what you think his or her comment and next question will be. You try to guide him or her. Or at least I do. In terms of relating this progression of ideas to music, I think I was exercising that habit in conversations before I was doing it with music. In every kind of venture, you have to try to discern where the other party's trying to go. If I'm in a deposition and the opposing attorney is asking all kinds of questions, I think to myself, "I'll answer this question by trying to anticipate what the question will be after the response I give him, because one thing leads to another."

Similarly, in listening to music, it is always fascinating to me how one chord leads to another, what the harmony leads to, and why. It is usually not fun for me when the harmony surprises me. It's not fun because it's a defeat; it didn't go the way I thought it was going. With each note or each chord, I am trying to anticipate what's next, and see what I think the composer intends. I hear the harmony change and I try to anticipate what the composer will then do. If my intuition proves to be accurate, I feel gratified.

Wagner's music, however, is a different experience. Listening to the harmonies in Wagner, I find it hard to predict what will come next. This difficulty in predicting the harmonies in Wagner sets him and his music apart from earlier composers, and yet I love his music. I dearly love it. Wagner's music can go a long time without harmonic resolution, and then resolution can come very suddenly. The long unresolved harmonies of Wagner play on my interest in concentration. I wouldn't say that Wagner seeks resolution with every succeeding note or combination of notes. Wagner's music is a continuous surprise because of the long delay in resolution, with notes after notes. He is always surprising me, more than most other composers. Consider Bach: you can almost always anticipate the next movement, and the same can be said of Handel's music. Being able to anticipate what's coming next is part of the joy of music for me. When I am not able to anticipate what harmonies come next, I'm frustrated. Then, my reaction is to concentrate more deeply on the music to see what I'm not catching, what I'm missing, and why. When I hear Wagner and the harmonies go places I did not anticipate, I experience a sense of frustration. However, despite this frustration, I love Wagner. He is a challenge for me, and I relish a challenge. All challenges are an opportunity to learn.

What I value above all in music is melody. The madrigals are the earliest music with which I am familiar. They have melody. The music that survives—that endures—always has melody. I cannot listen to the music of composers like Schoenberg. His compositions are noisy—full of dissonance, almost like a fight. I like peace and tranquility. Mozart elicits peace and tranquility. A Bach mass has a similar calming effect on me. Indeed, all music composed in reverence to God has a sedative effect. It is relaxing and yet inspires introspection. I listen endlessly to these chants and compositions of ages past, and I love them. They enrich me.

If there is one twentieth-century composer that will be heard a hundred years from now, it will be Gershwin. His music has more melody than the music of any other twentieth-century composer, with the possible exception of Richard Strauss. Mahler's music doesn't have as much melody. The same can be said about Copland's compositions. Stravinsky works usually don't have much of a melody, but *The Rite of Spring* does. Everything Gershwin wrote has melody. Likewise, everything Rachmaninoff wrote has melody. I love his music, especially his symphonies.

My performing in different groups and ensembles goes back to the time I was fifteen years old. I played my first string quartet, Haydn's *Kaiser Quartet,* in Lemon Grove, which was then a suburb of San Diego. Stuart Walker was the first violin, Leo Sheer the second violin, and Mary Ellen Thompson was the cellist. We sat out in a lemon grove and we played. It was a great experience. I also played string quartets with another group: Joe Kirshbaum was the first violinist, I was the second violinist, Ed Jenowski was the violist, and Arthur McBride was the cellist. I remember Joe, Ed, McBride, and I gave a concert, a recital, at the Thearle Music Company in downtown San Diego. We played with Stuart and Leo at the San Diego Art Museum in

Balboa Park. I was in a trio with a cellist whose name escapes me and Lois Wilson as the pianist, and we won a competition promoted by the *San Diego Sun*, the newspaper for which I later worked. Our pictures were in the paper.

I've played string quartets and trios regularly ever since those days. During my years at Antioch College, I played trios every week and quartets quite frequently on weekends in Winnetka and Chicago. In Winnetka, the cellist was sometimes William Lloyd. The pianist was Ada Chantney, the wife of a faculty member at Antioch, and she was quite a good pianist. We played trios together on weekends. I would go into Dayton, Ohio, to play string quartets with some friends of Ada, and I would stay there and play Saturday and Sunday. During summers I didn't stay in Antioch. I went back to San Diego and played in San Diego's "Symphonies under the Stars" program.

Later, when I was in Winnetka, I played quartets with Steve Staryk, who was then concertmaster with the Chicago Symphony. He was our first violinist. Henry Selinger was our second violinist. Joe Saunders was our cellist. We played frequently, and others played with us as substitutes. Frank Miller played with us. I played, too, with Milton Goldberg and Grace Nash.

I played at the Carmel Bach Festival for nineteen years. It wasn't nineteen successive years; I missed one or two summers. I auditioned for Sandor Salgo in the spring of 1957, and he accepted me as a member of the Carmel Bach Festival Orchestra, of which he was the musical director. Grace Nash, who was then teaching violin at the Dushkin School in Winnetka, knew about the Carmel Bach Festival through her sister who lived in the Bay Area. Grace told me that I ought to be playing in the festival. So, I called up Sandor Salgo and told him who I was, and that I'd like to audition for the viola section. He was game, so I went to his home and played for him, and he said he'd have a place for me. And he did: last stand inside. I never got beyond that place. But I loved it. I loved the rehearsals; I loved the music.

Also, in a contiguous village there was a conductors' workshop. The Ford and Rockefeller Foundations, I believe, jointly financed employment of an orchestra and an experienced senior conductor to administer the school. To conduct, you have to have an orchestra to lead. It was a six-week program. I would go occasionally and play in the viola section of that orchestra. Moreover, I became acquainted with the concertmaster of that orchestra, and we played quite a bit of chamber music. He and the cellist in our string quartet were on the faculty at the University of California, Santa Barbara. One year, during their spring vacation, the cellist rented a house in Acapulco for a couple of weeks, and we all went there and practiced string quartets. I had a wonderful time.

Then I decided that it was time for something new. I decided to take a month off every year and play string quartets instead of playing in the festival. The first year we played string quartets in Carmel. I rented a house on the 17-Mile Drive. The first violinist in that quartet was Polly Sweeney. Polly played in the Carmel Bach Festival, too, but when I quit, she also quit so we could do quartets together. Polly played chamber music with me for many, many years. I met her through Stuart Canin. She was Stuart's pupil. When my daughter Carol was at Aspen studying with Grant Johannesen, I met Stuart, who was then the concertmaster of the Aspen Orchestra. I remember lending him the "Earl of Darnley" Stradivarius violin when he was playing a Mozart concerto with the Aspen Orchestra. That loan was the beginning of a long association with Stuart. I played with him a great deal over many years. Some summers we managed to play all sixteen quartets of Beethoven, starting with Opus 18, Number 1, and continuing to Opus 135. I also enjoyed playing Brahms's quartets. I last played with Stuart and other friends in Saint-Tropez, in a beautiful house I rented in the summer of 1998. Danny Rothmuller was our cellist, and Rene Mandel, a student of Stuart's, was our second violinist.

After that memorable summer, I had an accident: my left index finger, all important for playing the viola, was caught in a car door I closed. No one else was responsible; it was my fault. I couldn't continue to play the viola. Still, I had a "good run." I played violin and viola for eighty years, from the age of seven to eighty-seven. By my own design, I was always the poorest player in the ensembles, usually quartets, in which I played. I always recognized that the better the player—or players—with whom I played, the better I played. When I would lose my place I used to say, "Man overboard!" I had gotten in trouble and had to call for help; we'd have to go back, ten measures or so, to fetch me aboard, and try again. Even though I was always "low man on the totem pole," I always enjoyed myself as much as anyone else, and—I suspect—probably more.

After my accident, I was only left with the opportunity to listen to music, and that I did. I have heard beautiful music in many places, ranging from my own home to such venues as New York's Lincoln Center. However, much of the great music I have heard has been in Salzburg, or an outgrowth of my visits to that charming Austrian city.

I first went to Salzburg in 1968 when I was making a quick circle-tour of Europe to see as much of it as I could in a limited period of time. I started out in London and crossed the Channel on a ferry. The first stop was Bruges, near Brussels. Then I went on to Amsterdam and through Germany. I lingered in a medieval village on the Rhine and explored Munich.

From Germany I went to Austria. Someone had spoken highly of Fuschl, so I went to Fuschl. I stayed at a lovely hotel, and the hotel concierge got tickets for a couple of evening performances at the Salzburg Festival. I drove into Salzburg, attended the performance, and drove back to the hotel for dinner. I did the same the next night. In two "back-to-back" evenings I heard what were, for me, great musical performances—I was impressed. Herbert von Karajan conducted both performances. On this very first visit, I also went up to the castle on the little tram. Then I continued my tour of Europe. I loved Salzburg, so I came back again the next summer. I think I may have attended four or five performances that year, and again I stayed out at Fuschl. Each year I stayed a bit longer and finally, after sixteen summers, I first rented Johannes and Sophie von Walderdorff's house high up on the Gaisberg. Johannes was the manager of the Hotel Goldener Hirsch in Salzburg. It is almost catty-corner from the Grosses Festspielhaus. Then, the following summer, I rented, from Dr. J. Franz and Isabelle Leibenfrost, the house that I've now had for twenty successive summers.

For many years the Salzburg Festival has stood as an icon in attracting an international audience to music performances during the summer months when, traditionally, the symphony orchestra and opera seasons elsewhere are dormant. I do worry, however, that the Salzburg Festival peaked a decade ago at the time of the death of Herbert von Karajan.

The summer of 2003 was my thirty-sixth successive year at Salzburg. I saw the Salzburg Festival in its glory, with top opera productions and fine musical presentations. Salzburg will be fortunate if it is able to maintain the high quality of musical performance that Hans Landesmann established, while bringing opera back to the excellence attained during the reign of Herbert von Karajan, and maintaining Gerard Mortier's accomplishment of greatly expanding the drama offerings of the festival. When I began attending the festival, there was only one play a year, with multiple performances. There could be, for example, a dozen presentations of *Jedermann*, the medieval morality play. Today, however, they offer a wide range of plays.

The summer of 2003 was the celebration of the 300th anniversary of the founding of St. Petersburg. In the company of good friends, I spent pleasant days at the Hermitage Museum and other museums, and even more pleasant evenings at the Mariinsky Theatre. There were lavish operas, symphonies, and ballet, all part of the aptly-named "White Nights Festival." When you come out of the theater at about eleven-thirty in the evening, you can see people sitting outside of restaurants having a cup of coffee and reading the newspaper. The sun sets at about three o'clock in the morning and rises only about two hours later.

For the last four years, I have celebrated my birthday in St. Petersburg, hosted by Valery Gergiev. He has a wonderful penthouse on the two top floors of a building facing the Neva River. It is beautiful to be there at a party, still going at two o'clock in the morning, and to see out of the windows the bridges going up across the Neva River. After the "White Nights Festival" in St. Petersburg, I go to Glyndebourne for two or three operas. Glyndebourne is about sixty-five miles south and a little bit east of London. Summer for me is a time to travel for the pleasure of hearing beautiful music.

A welcome but unexpected opportunity to listen to great music came from my support of the Los Angeles Philharmonic. Before the choice of Frank Gehry as architect for the Walt

Disney Concert Hall for the Los Angeles Philharmonic, I was invited to join a tour of the best acoustical halls in Europe. We went to halls in Great Britain, France, the Netherlands, and Germany. I enjoyed being in those halls and listening to the music being played. And I enjoyed the dialogue among various members of the tour as they expressed their thoughts and feelings. What I remember best, though, was Simon Rattle conducting his first performance of the Berlin Philharmonic. His father was in the audience. It was a great performance, and Rattle clearly made an unforgettable impression on the gifted musicians who make up the distinguished orchestra. I knew Rattle's father from earlier times, and I enjoyed seeing him again. I shared in his joy. His son's invitation was an immense honor—at that time the Berlin Philharmonic was widely regarded as the finest orchestra in the world. Seeing father and son united in the pride of accomplishment, I thought of the continuity of life and the way music ties together generations.

CHAPTER 8

# The Colburn School

IF I EVER HAD ANY doubt about the ability of any of us to take our possessions with us at the time of our demise, a visit to Egypt and the tombs of the pharaohs squelched that illusion. All of the riches and finery was still there in the tombs, untouched in the intervening centuries between the death of the pharaohs and the opening of the tombs. With that lesson in my mind (which was reinforced by my lawyer, Lou Hardin), I long ago decided to give away what I had earned and saved, above what I needed to enjoy a comfortable and happy life. After setting aside what the British call a "sufficiency," I brought into being several eleemosynary foundations whose mission is the teaching and performance of classical music on instruments employed during the periods of the composition, including music for the voice and to accompany classical dance.

I chose to give to music because that's where my love always has been. I initially was frustrated as a performer, but it was the best thing that could have happened because I had the benefit of playing music for love, not for money, virtually all my life, from the time I was seven until I was eighty-seven. I started giving to others when I was in my middle thirties. I gave money to music in different ways, including by buying instruments that I loaned to young people. My giving has continued, and it has increased with the passing years.

One of my early philanthropic acts was a gift in memory of Stuart Walker. Stuart was first violinist in the first string quartet in which I played. Leo Scheer was the second violinist, I was the violist, and Mary Ellen Thompson was the cellist. We played the *Kaiser Emperor Quartet* by Haydn—it was the first quartet I ever played. I was so happy. Stuart later graduated from the Yale School of Music. Sadly, Stuart died very young. I gave a contribution to Yale for the scholarship fund in his name.

An early gift that came to influence my most significant gifts—those that led to the establishment of the Colburn School—dates back to 1952 in Winnetka. David Dushkin, who ran a community music school there, decided to close the school and move to his summer home in Vermont, and make recorders full-time. He held a meeting on a Thursday with the four or five members of the faculty and announced that he was going to close the school. At that time, every Thursday evening I played with a string quartet that included Grace Nash as second violinist, who was also Dushkin's assistant. Having heard that day that Dushkin was closing the school, Grace, in the course of the evening, suggested that I invite some parents to join me in buying the house Dushkin owned so that the school could continue. My three children were in the school at the time.

Dushkin had an interesting philosophy about music education. He thought that every child should learn to play the recorder. Playing the recorder should be the beginning because it is simple to play. It is a means of learning to read notes, identify pitches and tones, and play tunes like "Three Blind Mice."

I persuaded three other parents to join me in carrying out Grace's wish. We established a nonprofit corporation to which we could contribute the funds necessary to buy the Dushkin home and school. After we bought the building, we learned that some neighbors went to the city council, which was also the zoning board, and protested that the transfer of the zoning variation to us was invalid. The neighbors felt that the zoning variation went with Dushkin as an individual, and not with the property. The village council accepted the views of the school's neighbors and wouldn't permit us to continue to operate the school at that location. So we sold the building, but we were given time to relocate the school. One of the board members of the new school's foundation was on the board of the North Shore Country Day School and prevailed upon that board to lease to the Music Center of the North Shore enough land for a school building and some parking space. Then we raised the necessary money and built a home for the school.

I said to Grace, "Well, Grace, who's going to run this school?" Grace said, "I think Herbert Zipper should be the one to do it." I said to Grace, "Who's Zipper?" I had never heard of Herbert Zipper. She told me about him and who he was. Zipper had been interned at Dachau and Buchenwald in Germany, fled to the Philippines—only to be interned there by the Japanese. Despite this hardship, Zipper emerged with boundless enthusiasm and energy—and a keen interest in music education.

Grace told me that Zipper was teaching at The New School for Social Research and living in New York. I said, "Well, get him out here and we'll talk to him and see if we can hire him." So, I flew him from New York to Chicago. Grace met him at the airport, brought him to the International Club at the Drake Hotel, where I met him, we dined, and I told him our story. He liked it, and he liked, too, the idea of coming to Winnetka. He said he would move, subject to the approval of his wife, Trudl. We quickly flew her out, as well, and she liked the idea, in part because it would also give her an opportunity to teach ballet, which would expand the school curriculum. So that's how I came to know Herbert Zipper.

Herbert then became director of the school, and was involved in the design and construction of the building. He built an apartment in the building for himself and Trudl. He lived at the school, and we were off and running. I didn't see a great deal of Herbert while he ran the school because he and I were both busy. He had a school to run and I had businesses to run, but, during those years, my daughter Carol studied piano and music theory with Herbert.

After I left Winnetka and moved to California, Herbert left the school. He received a grant from the Ford and Rockefeller Foundations to spend his time trying to bring into being community schools to focus on music education. This involved getting groups of parents together who would put up the money to establish music schools. He did that successfully for several years, but we were no longer in touch.

In the ensuing years, I was involved in providing support for and strengthening the management of many music-education and performance organizations. For example, Jim Arkatov and Joe Troy came to me with the idea of bringing into being a chamber orchestra for Los Angeles. I asked Joe who should be the conductor. Joe said, "Neville Marriner," and I said, "Who's he?" Joe loaned me a few of the recordings he had of the Academy of St. Martin-in-the-Fields chamber ensemble that Neville had brought into being, and that convinced me to engage him if possible. Neville was enticed to come out to Los

Angeles, and I thus helped establish the Los Angeles Chamber Orchestra.

About that time I established the Colburn Fund (which is distinct from the Colburn Music Fund) as a contribution vehicle for funds from various corporations in which I had an interest. The Colburn Fund helped bring into being more organizations, including the American Friends of the Bayreuth Festival, which supported the Richard Wagner Festival of Wagner's music, performed in the hall that he built. During this period I also helped establish the American Friends of Salzburg, known as the International Festival Society, which supports the Salzburg Festival. And I continued my support of select institutions, including prominently the Metropolitan Opera in New York and the Los Angeles Philharmonic.

In 1985, the Colburn Collection Foundation was established. This foundation helped formalize what had been an informal program of loaning to promising young musicians fine musical instruments I had collected over the years. At the time of the establishment of the Colburn Collection Foundation, there were seventy-two string instruments, a few of which were made by great masters, such as Stradivari, Amati, Guarneri, and Bergonzi. I have agreed to the suggestion of those who are overseeing the Colburn Collection that some of the high-value instruments should be sold with the proceeds being reinvested into the purchase of other instruments. When the value of instruments reaches a point where you're worried about their being taken on an airplane or being shoved into the back of a taxi, they really are not serving any charitable need. Prized violins can be put in a museum display case, but that is not a good thing for an instrument—they are meant to be played. And they should be played. The aspiration of the Colburn

Collection Foundation should be to have instruments that can all be loaned to promising young musicians.

My most significant gift to music, though, started a number of years earlier, in the late 1970s. It began with an unexpected telephone call, and would bring me back in touch with Herbert Zipper. The phone call came from Grant Beglarian, the dean of the School of Music and Performing Arts at the University of Southern California (USC). He asked if he might come and visit me, bringing with him Herbert Zipper. I said, "Well, I know Herbert well. Come on over and bring him along." So they came to visit. I knew Grant both as a dean and as a fellow violist. I had played chamber music a couple of times with him. He and Herbert came to visit me at my home in Beverly Hills. Grant told me that the USC Board of Trustees and the university's then-President John Hubbard had held a weekend retreat in Palm Springs for a line-by-line review of the budget because of the severe deficit that USC was facing in the current academic year. When they came to the performing arts preparatory school budget, Hubbard became aware for the first time that USC had a preparatory school. He "blew his top," saying, I am told, "What? A kindergarten? This is a university. We should close this preparatory school immediately."

Grant pleaded with Hubbard and the trustees to permit him to continue to operate the preparatory school through that academic year, saying it would be a tragedy to close it down and deprive the students of the performing arts training they were receiving. Grant said he thought that before the end of the school year he could find "a pigeon" who would take over the school so it would survive. Zipper suggested to Grant that I might be his pigeon. After some discussion, I said that in principle it sounded like something I would be willing to do, having done it before in Winnetka in a smaller way—and with Herbert. I gave a trusted assistant, Toby Mayman, the assignment of negotiating the deal with USC. From there on for the next twenty years, Toby was up to her ears in music education. She was not a musician herself, but she is intelligent and a quick learner, and she proved herself to be an outstanding administrator. Toby handled the discussions with USC. I can only remember attending one or two meetings. She negotiated the contract and I signed it.

As a result, in the fall of 1980, we took over the USC preparatory school of which Fran Zarubick was then director. Fran reported to Toby instead of to Grant, and Toby's education in music and school administration began. After a year or two, Fran had an opportunity to go to the preparatory school at the Peabody Institute, a school of music at Johns Hopkins University in Baltimore, Maryland. Toby's decision then to select Joe Thayer as Fran's successor was a good decision. Joe proved to be an exceedingly valuable assistant to Toby, and a strong administrator in running the day-to-day operations of the school. In 1999, when Toby elected to retire, Joe stepped into her place as executive director and has carried on brilliantly.

When we took the school over, it was operating in a Quonset hut at the southwest corner of the USC campus. Shortly thereafter, the then-named Community School of Performing Arts arranged to share the McMahon Brothers Furniture building and parking lot with USC's School of Music practice facility. This arrangement turned out well for both USC students and for the Community School, because the USC students took their lessons from nine in the morning until three o'clock in the afternoon. The Community School students didn't get out of their kindergarten, grade school, junior high, or high school classes until the midafternoon. They would take their lessons between three o'clock in the afternoon and nine o'clock at night. USC didn't have classes there on Saturdays or Sundays, so the Community School had the facility available all day on Saturdays and Sundays, which were the important days for the school at that location. It had a room that was marginally suitable for small recitals that we used regularly to give our students an opportunity to perform.

For the next fifteen years, Toby, Joe, and I continually looked for opportunities to relocate the school to more suitable facilities. I was approached to join with the Dance Gallery in leasing property from the Los Angeles Community Redevelopment Agency (CRA) and building a facility to accommodate the Dance Gallery and our school. This would have solved the school's short-range space problems. I committed myself to advancing necessary funds, but the project never came to fruition. Soon thereafter, in the early 1990s, Ed Edelman, a member of the school's board and a former Los Angeles County supervisor, suggested seeking other property from the CRA. Ed was highly respected and well connected politically. Negotiations shifted to a parcel of land on the east side of Grand Avenue, just north of the Museum of Contemporary Art. As a result, the school ended up with an excellent parcel of land. Ed worked with Toby and officials of the CRA to obtain the present land-lease arrangement plus the option for the western half of the square block bounded by the west on Grand Avenue; the east by Olive Street; north being 2nd Street; and south being General Thaddeus Kosciuszko Way. Planning for the new school facility began in 1994. Toby and Joe were primarily responsible for overseeing the design and construction of the school. They participated in meetings where we selected the architects. Four architects submitted drawings and models. Hardy Holzman Pfeiffer Associates was selected unanimously by the board. Construction was completed in 1998.

Toby persuaded me in 1986 that I should be more open about my support for the school, and that I acquiesce to a suggestion that members of the board were making: that the school be named the Richard D. Colburn School of Performing Arts. I did agree, and so my name was put on the new building. My daughter Carol suggested that the school's concert hall be named Zipper Hall. All agreed. In time, a smaller hall was named Mayman Hall. Later, when talk began of expanding—someday—the school to include a full-fledged conservatory, I decided that the school would be better named just the Colburn School. I hoped that other family members—my children—would continue what I had started—building a world-class music school on the West Coast of the United States.

In July of 1998, the school moved from near USC to its new location at Grand Avenue, one block south of the Music Center. This move was just prior to the groundbreaking for the Walt Disney Concert Hall in 2001, diagonally across Grand Avenue from the school. When I took over the preparatory school from USC, the school had about 200 students. It was a preparatory school, distinct from the USC School of Performing Arts. By 2002, the Colburn School had about 1,300 students.

Historically, in Western Europe and the United States, music education has been split into two parts: so-called preparatory schools that instruct young people in music through their high school years and then so-called conservatories that pick up at that point and continue the training. This artificial division doesn't make sense. Some young gifted people will play violin better at twelve than others will ever play, no matter how long they attend a conservatory. And with the conservatory approach, students are sometimes not exposed early enough to a broad range of related subjects: composition, harmony, counterpoint, the character and ranges of the various instruments of the orchestra, and the history of music.

A few blocks from my London home in Chester Square, there is a plaque that reads, "Mozart composed his first symphony here at age eight." If he could compose a symphony at eight, he had to have learned something about composition, harmony, counterpoint, the character of sound, and the tonal range of the instruments of an orchestra. That's a lot of learning to have packed into eight years. But his father was a music teacher and taught in his home. So, from the day of his conception to his leaving the womb, he heard music virtually every day, all day. In his sleep, he probably still heard music. It was quite natural for him to exhibit curiosity about music, as well as about other aspects of life. So, his father trained him at an early age.

One rarely finds in America or Western Europe any student studying composition, harmony, or counterpoint at age six. It just doesn't happen. But, when a child is young and eager to learn, why shouldn't he or she be taught? One needs to ask why, during the 240 years since Mozart, no symphony of notable maturity has been composed by an eight-year-old. It is not likely to happen under the present system of music education in Western Europe and the United States. So I have proposed for the Colburn School that we abolish from our vocabulary the expression "preparatory school" in talking about music education. We're going to talk about a "music school." If a child wants to study composition at age six, we're going to teach him or her at age six. If students want to study counterpoint and harmony at an early age, we're going to teach them at that age. In the first year of life, a child's mind absorbs more than he or she will learn in any other year of life.

We should think of music education as a "tutorial," which it is, with every student progressing at his or her own pace. If a student wants to learn to write music at age six, teach him or her at age six. Why not? If students meet the qualifications for a degree at age twelve, why not give them a degree instead of giving it to them when they are nineteen, twenty, twenty-two, or twenty-three years old? Waiting is nonsensical. The individual approach is going to prevail in the Colburn School. In the fall of 2003, the school expanded its academic program to embrace the teaching of composition, harmony, counterpoint, and other subjects required to qualify the school as a degree-granting institution under the standards of the National Association of Schools of Music, and to be licensed by the State of California. I hope that the whole of society will benefit from the Colburn School. Wouldn't Mozart have loved to be at such a music school?

Printed in Great Britain
by Amazon

60777353R00080